Anne Frank Huis
Amsterdam

Otto Frank's office building, 263 Prinsengracht (centre), around 1947.

Otto Frank's office building can be seen in this aerial photo from 1949. The front and back sections of the building are clearly marked.

The back of 263 Prinsengracht, 1954. The Secret Annexe inhabitants lived on the second and third floors. The uppermost window is that of the Annexe attic.

The view from the window of the Secret Annexe attic, 2005. Anne mentions the chestnut tree several times in her diary.

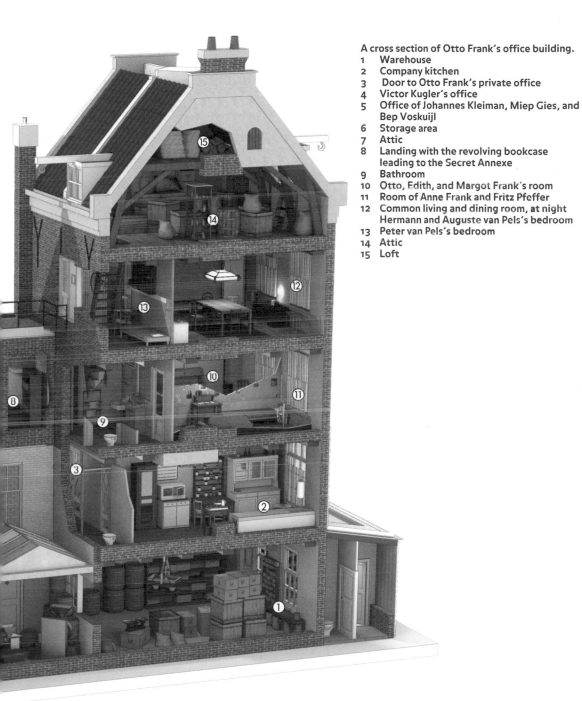

A cross section of Otto Frank's office building.

1 Warehouse
2 Company kitchen
3 Door to Otto Frank's private office
4 Victor Kugler's office
5 Office of Johannes Kleiman, Miep Gies, and
   Bep Voskuijl
6 Storage area
7 Attic
8 Landing with the revolving bookcase
   leading to the Secret Annexe
9 Bathroom
10 Otto, Edith, and Margot Frank's room
11 Room of Anne Frank and Fritz Pfeffer
12 Common living and dining room, at night
   Hermann and Auguste van Pels's bedroom
13 Peter van Pels's bedroom
14 Attic
15 Loft

Anne Frank, 16 July 1941.

A long line in front of the employment office in Hannover, 1932. In February 1932 more than six million Germans (20%) are unemployed. On the wall are the words 'Wählt Hitler' (Vote for Hitler).

Members of the SA (Sturmabteilung), the NSDAP commando unit, marching through Berlin, 1932.

Hitler is appointed Chancellor and waves to an enthusiastic crowd in Berlin, 30 January 1933.

NSDAP followers, including many students, burn books by Jewish writers and political opponents in Berlin on 10 May 1933. The same thing happens in many other German cities on the same day.

A large NSDAP rally in Berlin, August 1935. The banners read 'Die Juden sind unser Unglück!' (The Jews are our misfortune) and 'Frauen und Mädchen, die Juden sind Euer Verderben' (Women and girls, the Jews are your downfall).

The burning synagogue in Bielefeld, Germany, during 'Kristallnacht', 9 – 10 November 1938.

A demolished Berlin shop, 10 November 1938.

Adolf Hitler greets the soldiers of the Condor Legion after their return from the Spanish Civil War, 6 June 1939.

German soldiers examine the remains of a Polish army column after an attack by German planes, 20 September 1939.

A crashed German plane between Rotterdam and Delft, May 1940.

The commander of a German tank asks for directions; a Dutch boy looks on, 1940.

The centre of Rotterdam after the German air attack of 14 May 1940. When the Germans threaten to bomb Utrecht and other cities as well, the Dutch army capitulates.

On 16 May 1940 Germany army units pass through the centre of Amsterdam. This photo was taken right near Otto Frank's office building.

Anka Nienhuis-Szymelmic sews a Star of David onto her coat, Amsterdam, 1944 or 1945.

Three Jewish girls in Utrecht, 1942. These are the twin sisters Sophia (left) and Haddassa Wijzenbeek (right). The name of their girlfriend is unknown.

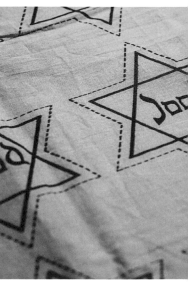

Stars of David on a piece of cloth. Jews were given a maximum of four and had to pay for them.

Anne's father, Otto Frank, is not at home when the call-up notice is delivered. So Edith Frank goes to get Hermann van Pels. He is a friend of the family who works at Otto Frank's company, and he lives nearby. She tells Anne and Margot not to open the door to anyone.

Margot tells her sister that a call-up notice has come for their father. Anne is shocked and doesn't know what to do. Suddenly someone else comes to the door. It's Hello again, but Anne and Margot keep quiet and don't answer it. When Edith Frank comes back later with Hermann van Pels, she sends Margot and Anne to their room. She needs some time alone with Hermann to plan their next move.

The call-up notice for Margot didn't just drop out of the sky. Rumours had already been spreading that all Jews would be forced to leave the Netherlands. So Otto and Edith Frank have been making preparations and asking for reliable help, should it ever become necessary.

While they're waiting in their room, Margot tells Anne that the call-up is for her and not for their father. Anne bursts into tears. Margot tries to comfort her. Of course she's not going to Germany all by herself; she's going to go into hiding, along with the entire family. To keep themselves occupied they start picking out things they'll want to take with them to the hiding place.

While packing everything in her schoolbag, Anne wonders where the hiding place is: 'in the city, in the countryside, in a house, in a hut?' *I*

After a while the telephone rings. It's Jacqueline, Anne's friend from school. Anne's mother has told her not to say anything suspicious, so the call is a short one. At five o'clock Otto Frank comes home. Hermann van Pels goes to see Jan and Miep Gies to inform them of the situation. The couple are friends of the Frank family; Miep is also an employee in Otto Frank's business. Hermann asks if they would help carry as many things as possible to the hiding place. In the meantime, Otto Frank calls another company employee, Johannes Kleiman, with the same request. Until late in the evening, the helpers go in and out of the Frank family's home to help them make the secret move.

Anne is exhausted by the time she goes to bed at eleven-thirty, and she falls asleep as soon as her head hits the pillow. The next morning Edith wakes her up at five-thirty. She tells Anne to put on as many clothes as she can, because walking through the streets with a suitcase would draw too much attention. Fortunately it's raining cats and dogs, so there are fewer German soldiers outside.

Miep Gies comes to fetch Margot. They leave for the hiding place by bicycle. It has to appear as

mijn grootmoeder en wil dat ik naar
Ursul ga, en niet naar jou, maar ik ben
dat niet van mening en ook niet van
plan, oude mensen hebben soms erg ouderwet-
se begrippen, maar daar hen ik me niet naar
richten. Ik heb me grootouders wel
nodig, maar ik weet, zij hebben mij
toch ook nodig. Zo heb ik woensdags avonds
altijd vrij, omdat ik voor mijn grootouders naar handwerkles ga, maar ik ga
naar zo'n clubje van de zionistische
partij, dat mag ik niet omdat mijn
grootouders erg tegen het zionisme
zijn. Ik ben er ook niet fanatiek voor,
maar ik voel er wel wat voor, en
ik interesseer me er voor.
Maar de laatste tijd is het dan zo'n
rommelkoortje dat ik van plan ben
er niet te gaan, en daarom is Woensdagavond de laatste avond dat ik er naar
toe ga. Dan ben ik dus Woensdagavond,
Vrijdagavond, Zaterdagmiddag, Zondagmiddag en al. zo meer.
"Maar als je grootouders het nu niet
willen, dan moet jij het toch niet achter
hun rug doen."

wonder boven wonder, ben ik niet meteen
de trap afgesuisd, maar heb rus-
tig afgewacht tot hij gebeld heeft.
Ik ging naar beneden, en hij ging mee-
teen met de deur in huis.
"Zeg Anne, mijn grootmoeder vindt jou
nog te jong, om geregeld met ons te
gaan, en ze zegt dat ik naar Löwen-
bachs moet gaan, maar je weet misschien, dat ik niet meer met Ursul om-
ga."
"Nee, hoezo, hebben jullie ruzie gehad?"
"Nee, integendeel ik heb juist tegen Ursul
gezegd dat we toch niet goed met elkaar op konden schieten, en dat we daarom maar niet meer met elkaar om
moesten gaan, maar dat Ursul bij ons
nog best welkom was, en dat ik hoopte
dat ik dat ook bij haar was. Ik dacht
namelijk dat Ursul met een andere jongen
handelde en heb haar daar ook naar ge-
handeld. Maar dat was helemaal niet
waar, en nu ging mijn om dat ik Ursul excuus moest aanbieden, maar dat
wilde ik natuurlijk niet en daarom heb
ik, het uit gemaakt, maar dat was maar
er van de vele redenen.

/ 31

/ 30

Anne writes in this diary for the first time on her thirteenth
birthday. Six months later it's full. These diary pages were written
on 1 July 1942.

This is the diary Anne is given for her thirteenth birthday.

Open >

Otto Frank and Edith Holländer with their
wedding guests on 12 May 1925.

Otto and Edith spend their honeymoon in San
Remo, Italy.

Otto and Edith going for a stroll in Frankfurt am Main, March 1927. From left to right: Edith Frank with Margot, cousin Bernd Elias in a baby carriage, a nursemaid, cousin Stephan Elias, and Otto Frank.

Edith Frank with Margot, 1929.

Otto Frank with Margot and Anne, 1931.

A little photo of Edith, Anne, and Margot from
the photo machine of the Tietz department
store, 10 March 1933. Together they weigh 110
kilos.

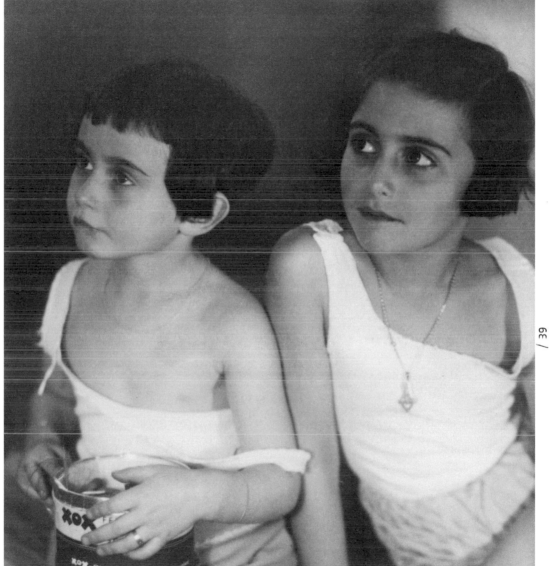

Margot and Anne spend a couple of months with
Grandma Holländer in Aachen at the end of 1933
while their mother looks for a place to live in
Amsterdam.

Margot and Anne in Aachen, 1933.

Margot Frank, 1935.

Maak Uwe
Fyne Vruchten-Jam
Marmelade en Gelei

zelf in 10 minuten

met **Opekta**

geheel uit Vruchten bereid

RECEPTENBOEKJE

voor het bereiden van

Jams en Geleiën

in 10 minuten

met opekta

VLOEIBAAR

N.V. Nederl. Opekta Mij. Prinsengracht 263 Amsterdam-C Tel. 37059

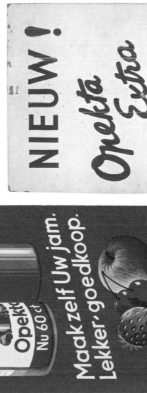

NIEUW !

Opekta Extra

Een nieuwe kwaliteit met
sterker geleervermogen.

Inkoopprijs 67½ ct. per flesje.

Publieksprijs 95 ,, ,, ,,

Maak zelf Uw jam.
Lekker, goedkoop.

Nu 60 ct

Otto Frank's company sells Opekta, a pectin compound used in making jam. Otto Frank's company – Opekta – moves into the premises at 263 Prinsengracht in December 1940.

/ 41

/ 42 Anne Frank made these drawings in her last year at the 6th Montessori School.

A poem by Anne Frank in the album of verses belonging to her girlfriend Juultje Ketellapper. Juultje was killed in Sobibor in 1943 along with her parents and her little sister.

In order to keep his companies out of the hands of the German occupiers, Otto Frank transfers the directorship to his employees, Johannes Kleiman and Victor Kugler.

Handelsregister van de Kamer van Koophandel en Fabrieken

VOOR ...... NOORD-HOLLAND ....

UITTREKSEL uit de opgaaf van ...de Naamlooze Vennootschap: N.V.HANDELSVER-

EENIGING GIES & CO., ... gevestigd te ...... Amsterdam-C.,
.... Prinsengracht 263 .

Ingeschreven onder N°. .... 56645 ....

Als Directeur is in de opgaaf vermeld:
VICTOR GUSTAV KUGLER, wonende te Hilversum, Eemnesserweg 56, ge-
boren te Hohenelbe (Dld) 6 Juni 1900, nationaliteit Nederlandsche.
(Genat.27 Mei 1938).
Als Waarnemend Directeur komt in de opgaaf voor:
JOHANNES KLEIMAN, wonende te Amsterdam, Wielingenstraat 12 II, ge-
boren te Koog a/d. Zaan, 17 Augustus 1896, nationaliteit Nederl.

Aan

de N.V. Handelsvereeniging Gies & Co.,
.... Prinsengracht 263,
te .... AMSTERDAM (C)

-Als-

[Mod. 16a.] [Uittreksel halffolio.]

K 1004

**Margot and Anne with their girlfriends, around
1934. From left to right: Anne, Ellen Weinberger,
Margot, and Gabrielle Kahn.**

Anne Frank, 1935.

Anne with her girlfriends Eva Goldberg and
Sanne Ledermann on the Merwedeplein, 1936.

Anne with her teacher, Miss Godron, and her
classmates Martha van den Berg (left) and Rela
Salomon (right), 1940.

A class photo of Anne from the 6th Montessori School, 1938

Anne (second from left) in Vondel Park in
Amsterdam, winter of 1940-1941. Figure skating
is her great passion. This is the only surviving
skating photo of Anne.

The Frank family on the Merwedeplein, 1941.

Anne stays with the Ledermann family in a
pension in Beekbergen during the summer
vacation, June 1941. From left to right: Anne,
Tineke Gatsonides, Sanne and Barbara
Ledermann.

Anne in her last year of primary school, 1940.

3
'I'm a nervous wreck'

/ 9 October 1942

6 July 1942 —
December 1942

When the Frank family arrive at the Secret
Annexe on July 6th they're confronted by total
chaos. Boxes, food, dishes, and furniture are all
mixed up together. The family spend their first
days hard at work, unpacking and arranging
things. Anne and her father immediately start
working on makeshift curtains so the neighbours
won't be able to see inside. The Secret Annexe
consists of two floors and an attic. One floor is
for the Frank family and the other is set aside for
the Van Pels family. The attic is not suitable for
human habitation; it's damp, and rats live there.

During the day the Annexe inhabitants have
to wear slippers and keep their voices down,
since there are people working in the warehouse
who must not find out that anyone is hiding
there. The drainpipe for the Secret Annexe toilet
runs right through the warehouse. This means

that during the day use of the toilet must be kept to a minimum.

After the Frank family have been in the Secret Annexe for a week, Hermann and Auguste van Pels arrive with their son Peter and the cat Mouschi. Hermann van Pels has been spreading the rumour throughout the neighbourhood that the Frank family have fled to Switzerland, and everyone thinks it's true. The Franks have a good laugh: if only the neighbours knew how close they really were. Anne knows Peter van Pels. When she turned thirteen he came over to congratulate her. She's not very excited about having him around. In her diary she calls him a 'rather boring and shy beanpole', *I* and in the beginning she's even a little afraid of Mouschi the cat.

14 August 1942

During those first few months in particular Anne longs for her own cat, Moortje, whom she had to leave behind. But she also thinks a lot about her girlfriends. In late September Anne writes a goodbye letter in her diary to her school friend Jacqueline. Unfortunately she can't mail the letter because it's too dangerous. But Anne pretends Jacqueline has answered her, and she writes her a second letter.

Because the Secret Annexe inhabitants have to be so quiet during the day, Anne does a lot of reading. Her very favourite books are the ones by

Cissy van Marxveldt. They're all about the adventures of the lively Joop ter Heul and her club of girlfriends. Anne misses her own girlfriends, and in her diary she pretends to be corresponding with the girlfriends of Joop ter Heul: Jet, Kitty, Emmy, Marianne, Conny, Pien, Pop, and Lou. Besides reading and doing the necessary household chores, Anne spends a great deal of time on her schoolwork. She has absolutely 'no intention of still being in the first class when I'm 14 or 15'. /

When it comes to food, books, newspapers, magazines, and anything else the Annexe inhabitants might need, they're completely dependent on the helpers: Miep Gies, Johannes Kleiman, Victor Kugler, and Bep Voskuijl. Jan Gies also becomes involved. There are other people who help as well: the butcher, the baker, the milkman, and the greengrocer sell them whatever they need without asking any questions, and sometimes they even make deliveries. The helpers are also able to obtain extra ration coupons through middlemen. Many provisions are being rationed and cannot be bought without coupons.

Usually Miep Gies comes in the morning to make up a shopping list. At noon – when the warehouse workers are on their break – the helpers often join the Annexe inhabitants for lunch and to keep them company. All this time their work for the business continues as usual. 'We had to seem perfectly relaxed to the outside world or people would have become suspicious,' Miep says after the war. /

In the evening the helpers and the other personnel go home and the Annexe inhabitants have the place all to themselves. Only then – and in the weekend when no one is there – can they leave the Secret Annexe and visit other parts of the building. They might go to the director's office, for example, to listen to the radio. The first time they leave the Annexe, Anne is terrified; all she wants to do is go back to the safety of the hiding place as soon as possible. Her mother understands her fear and goes back with her.

Because Anne is so insistent, Miep and Jan Gies as well as Bep Voskuijl come to spend a night in the Secret Annexe. It's fun for the Annexe inhabitants, but the helpers don't sleep a wink. As Miep Gies later recalls, 'The fright of these people who were locked up here was so thick I could feel it pressing down on me. It was like a thread of terror pulled taut. It was so terrible it never let me close my eyes. For the first time I knew what it was like to be a Jew in hiding.' /

The Annexe inhabitants have to rely on their helpers for news from the city. The news is bad.

Menno Metselaar, *Anne Frank Magazine*, 1998

Miep Gies, *Anne Frank Remembered: The Story of the Woman Who Helped to Hide the Frank Family*, 1987

Jews have to report their whereabouts, and those who don't are picked up and put on transport. Bep tells Anne that Betty Bloemendal, a girl from her class, has been taken to occupied Poland. She thinks about Peter Schiff, her big crush, and wishes he'd come hide in the Secret Annexe too. But maybe he's already dead...

1 August 1942 'I'm so scared that we'll be discovered and shot,' *I* Anne writes in her diary in August. The windows of the company that look out on the Secret Annexe are covered over or painted so you can't see through them. Victor Kugler comes up with the idea of putting a bookcase in front of the door to the Secret Annexe to make it look as if there were no Annexe at all. He asks Johan Voskuijl, Bep's father, to build such a bookcase. Johan Voskuijl works in the warehouse. At first he wasn't told about the hiding place, but soon he was let in on the secret. For the inhabitants it's reassuring to know that he's in the warehouse keeping an eye on things, because the other employees working there must never find out what's going on.

In the autumn of 1942 an eighth Jewish person comes to hide in the Secret Annexe. Fritz Pfeffer is an acquaintance of the Frank family. He's a dentist and he's just as old as Otto Frank, 53. His girlfriend Charlotte Kaletta is not Jewish, so she doesn't have to go into hiding. Margot moves into her parents' room and Anne has to share her room with this new inhabitant.

Fritz Pfeffer is astonished to find the Frank family in the Secret Annexe. Like many of the Franks' neighbours, he assumed that the family had fled to Switzerland by way of Maastricht. Anne doesn't like having to share her room with him, but she has no choice.

Fritz Pfeffer tells them the latest news of the Frank family's friends and acquaintances. None of the reports are good. The German police – often helped by Dutch officers – have arrested hundreds of Jews and put them on transport to Westerbork transit camp in Drente and from there to occupied Poland. The Annexe inhabits fear the worst and think 'that most of them have been killed'. **/** The BBC, which they listen to, has even said something about 'gassing'. **/** 'I'm a nervous wreck,' **/** Anne writes in her diary. 9 October 1942

The helpers try to cheer them up. They organise a secret Sinterklaas party for the inhabitants on 5 December. Only Otto Frank knows about it. The helpers have made presents and written funny poems for all of them, which they put in a large basket and leave in the office. The inhabitants are quite impressed when they later hear that Johan Voskuijl made a number of the presents himself: bookends, a picture frame, and an ashtray. One year later Anne still fondly looks back on the party.

In August 1942 a revolving bookcase is built to hide the entrance to the Secret Annexe. This photo was taken in 1999.

A photo of the bookcase from 1954. A map of Belgium covers the hole at the top.

The revolving bookcase is temporarily removed in the fifties. This photo clearly shows that a small step had to be taken out first before the bookcase could be put in place.

In 1998 the Secret Annexe is temporarily furnished for the making of a film. This is Mr and Mrs Van Pels's bedroom, which also served as the common living room.

The Secret Annexe kitchen, temporarily refurnished, 1990.

This is what the Secret Annexe kitchen looked like in 1954.

The Secret Annexe inhabitants
(from left to right)

Otto Frank, around 1938.
Edith Frank, May 1935.
Margot Frank, May 1942.
Anne Frank, May 1942.
Auguste van Pels, July 1941.
Hermann van Pels, July 1941.
Peter van Pels, 1942.
Fritz Pfeffer, around 1939.

The helpers
(from left to right)

Miep Santrouschitz. She marries Jan Gies
on 16 July 1941.
Bep Voskuijl, 1945.
Johannes Kleiman.
Victor Kugler, the thirties.
Johan Voskuijl, Bep's father, early thirties.
Jan Gies, early forties.

**Otto with the helpers, October 1945. From left to
right: Miep Gies, Johannes Kleiman, Otto Frank,
Victor Kugler, and Bep Voskuijl.**

The director's office is temporarily refurnished, 1998.

The helpers use these stairs to make their way unseen from the office to the hiding place.

The director's office in the fifties.

The office of Johannes Kleiman, Miep Gies, and Bep Voskuijl.

Some of the office personnel in 1941. From left to right: Victor Kugler, Esther, Bep Voskuijl, Pine Wuurman, and Miep Gies. Esther's last name is unknown. By 1942 Esther and Pine are no longer working at Opekta.

4
FEAR

The inhabitants of the Secret Annexe live in constant fear of discovery. Neighbours, warehouse employees, company visitors: no one must ever notice anything. 'How easily a little carelessness can give you away!' *I* Anne writes in her diary. Anne also realises that the helpers are anxious and worried as well. But at least they can go to the movies every now and then, take a day trip, have a party, and even go on vacation.

18 May 1943

During the first months the helpers tell the Annexe inhabitants all the news from the outside world, but they begin holding back when they notice how despondent this makes them. After the war Miep Gies says, 'Jan, my husband, told me, "Miep, you mustn't always tell them everything. You have to keep in mind that these people are locked up. They can't go outside. Bad news depresses them even more than it does us. Try to tell them half good news and half bad."' *I*

Menno Metselaar, *Anne Frank Magazine*, 1998

The inhabitants are mainly afraid of dogfights and bombings. After all, they can't go anywhere. All they can do is wait and hope for the best. Anne becomes especially anxious when German anti-aircraft guns fire on Allied planes. 'I still haven't gotten over my fear of anything that shoots or flies, and almost every night I crawl into bed next to father for comfort. That may sound very childish, but wait till it happens to you. You can hardly hear yourself think with all the guns roaring.' **/**

10 March 1943

A new danger arises when food and household provisions in the occupied Netherlands become scarce. The number of break-ins increases. Apparently the firm on the Prinsengracht is an attractive target for thieves. After a break-in occurs in April 1944, a policeman comes to take a look. When he pulls on the bookcase the Annexe inhabitants hold their breath. But fortunately he soon gives up.

From her diary we learn that Anne has a particularly hard time with Sundays, which are long days indeed. None of the helpers are there to visit them and the Annexe inhabitants are completely on their own. 'I (...) go lie down on the divan and sleep to try to reduce the time, the silence, and terrible anxiety, because it's impossible to kill it.' **/** Sometimes her fear turns into a feeling of indifference: 'I've come to the point where I don't care whether I die or keep on living.' **/**

29 October 1943

3 February 1944

Anne reports in her diary that she takes valerian pills 'for anxiety and depression'. **/** She herself is convinced that humour is the best

16 September 1943

medicine for keeping her anxiety under control. 'A good, hearty laugh would be more helpful than 10 valerian pills.' **/** But that's not easy when you've been locked up for more than a year without ever being able to go outside.

16 September
1943

Anne finds comfort in nature more than anything else. 'I know I'm not imagining it, but seeing the sky, the clouds, the moon, and the stars calms me down and makes me hopeful. It's a much better remedy than valerian or bromide. Nature makes me know my little place in the vast universe and gives me the courage to meet any blow!' **/** Anne also derives strength from her belief in God. After a year and a half in hiding she finally works up the courage to go to the warehouse on her own. She hears the threatening roar of airplanes but she is no longer afraid. Anne places her fate in the hands of God.

13 June 1944

5

'The cockiest girl in the world'

/ 11 July 1943

January — July 1943

Life in the Secret Annexe is not easy for Anne. She's the youngest, and everyone has something to say about her. At the end of January 1943 she writes in her diary in despair, 'I'd like to scream at Mother, Margot, V.P., Pf., and even Father: "Leave me alone, let me finally get a good night's sleep without my pillow being wet with tears (...). Let me go away, away from everything, especially away from the world!" But I can't. I can't let them see how desperate I feel.' *I*   30 January 1943

Anne often feels very alone. She fills her days with studying, reading, and writing. In addition to her school subjects Anne is also taking a stenography course. Stenography is a handy way of quickly writing down what someone is saying. Anne is especially enthusiastic about reading. She looks forward to Saturdays, when Miep Gies brings the Annexe inhabitants five new library books.

Anne can pour out her feelings by writing in her diary. At this point she's addressing her diary letters to only one of the friends of *Joop ter Heul*: Kitty. She often writes about quarrels in those letters. The atmosphere in the Secret Annexe is frequently so tense you could cut it with a knife. 'The whole house is thundering with arguments. Mother and me, V.P. and Papa, Mother and Madam, everybody's mad at everybody. Nice atmosphere, isn't it?' / When Fritz Pfeffer first arrives at the Secret Annexe he tries to mediate between the various parties, but he soon gives up.

27 April 1943

Anne and her mother don't always get along. On one occasion Edith asks Anne to pray with her before going to sleep and Anne refuses. She'd rather pray with her father. Anne knows that this has hurt her mother deeply. 'She cried half the night and hardly got any sleep.' / Anne's father is angry and thinks she should apologise, but Anne stubbornly refuses.

2 April 1943

Fortunately it's not all quarrelling in the Secret Annexe. The inhabitants try to get through the long days as pleasantly as they can. All the birthdays and holidays are festively celebrated with presents again and again. The inhabitants treat each other from their own rations, and they ask the helpers to buy things for them. In early 1943 there are also rays of hope in the outside world. The German army loses the Battle of Stalingrad, and thousands of soldiers are taken prisoner. There are more and more Allied air attacks of major German cities. Allied planes flying over Amsterdam are regularly fired on by German anti-aircraft guns. Although the Annexe inhabitants are happy about the Allied activities, the noise of the German ack-acks often robs them of their sleep. Anne is worn out and has dark rings under her eyes.

At the end of March 1943, Dutch resistance fighters carry out an attack on the Amsterdam city registry. The registry is where the personal data of everyone living in Amsterdam is kept. If these papers are destroyed, it's difficult for the Nazis to track people down. The attack fails. There is some damage, but most of the administration remains intact.

The Annexe inhabitants often wonder how long the war is going to go on. In May 1943, Hermann van Pels, whom Anne thinks has a good grasp of the situation, says he believes the war won't be over until the end of that year. That seems like a long time to her, but Anne remains optimistic. The inhabitants will surely make it through eight more months.

On 12 June 1943 Anne turns fourteen. It's her first birthday in the Secret Annexe. Anne gets lots of presents, such as a book about Greek and

The room of Anne Frank and Fritz Pfeffer in 1954.

Anne pastes all sorts of pictures on the walls of her room. Some of them even overlap. During her years in hiding her interest shifts from movie stars and royalty to art.

POLDERLANDSCHAP
LANGS DE EEM BIJ BAARN

Anne pasted a photo of Michelangelo's Pietà over a picture of the Hollywood stars Priscilla and Rosemary Lane.

Anne had a knock-down battle with Fritz Pfeffer over the use of the little table in their room, which she worked into a short story.

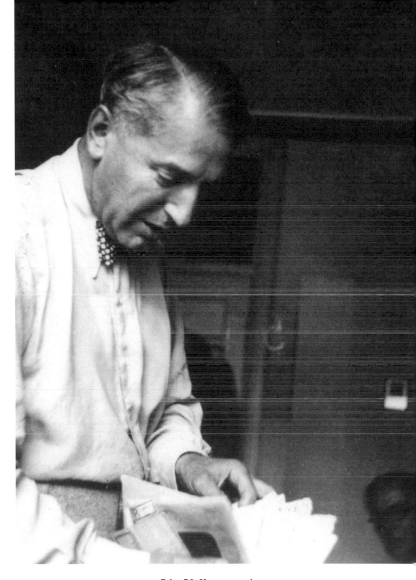

Fritz Pfeffer, around 1939.

The room of Anne Frank and Fritz Pfeffer is temporarily refurnished, 1998.

View from Anne Frank's room in 1954.

In the fifties, plans were made to pull the building down. As a precaution, Otto Frank cut out Anne's pictures and put them in safekeeping.

Maandag 27 December 1943.
Vrijdagavond heb ik voor
het eerst in mijn leven iets
voor Kerstmis gekregen.
De meisjes, Kleiman en
Kugler hadden weer een heerlijke verrassing voorbe-
reid. Miep heeft een heerlijke Kerstkoek gebakken,
waar "Vrede 1944" opstond. Een pond boterkoekjes
van vooroorlogse kwaliteit bezorgde Bep.

Voor Peter, Margot
flesje yoghurt en
elk een bier.
Luck ingepakt en
Ze waren op de
potten geplakt.
Zijn voor ons, ieder jaar

en mij was er een
van de volwassenen.
Alles was weer zo
deze leuke plaat-
verschillende pak-
De Kerstdagen
voorbijgegaan.

Anne.

When Anne's plaid diary is full, she continues her writing in various notebooks. Not all of them have been saved. This notebook covers the period 22 December 1943 through 17 April 1944.

haar is vergeten. Nooit zal hij dit vergeten.
Hij is toegevend geworden! want ook hij
liet moeders fouten. Ik hoop dat ik een beetje
op hem ga lijken, zonder dat ik dat ook moet
doormaken!   je
                Anne.

/ 93

/ 96

Open >

Peter van Pels, 1942. In one of her short stories, 'My First Interview', Anne pretends to be interviewing him, and she describes his room in detail.

Anne Frank, May 1941.

ENGLEBER
A.D

Peter van Pels's room, temporarily refurnished,
1998. Anne envies Peter his privacy.

Peter's room in 1954. In one of her short stories
Anne writes that she gave him a couple of
pictures of movie stars to brighten up his room.

The stock market game that Peter is given
for his sixteenth birthday on 8 November 1942.

The Annexe attic window in 1954. Anne and Peter could be alone here and talk together. Anne also came here to get a breath of fresh air.

The stairs to the attic in Peter's room, 1954. Because of these, Anne calls it a 'walk-through room'.

The Annexe attic is temporarily refurnished, 1998.

Auguste and Hermann van Pels, 1941.

The common living room, temporarily refurnished, 1998. In the summer of 1943 the Annexe inhabitants begin listening to the radio here.

Herrn Erich Elias,

Herbstgasse 11

B a s e l . Schw.

N.V. Ned. Opekta Mij.
PRINSENGRACHT 263
(bij de Westertoren)
AMSTERDAM-C.
TELEFOON 37059

Amsterdam, 8.September 1943

Sehr geehrter Herr Elias,

    Nur einige Zeilen um Ihnen zu sagen,dass es uns allen gut geht. Geschäftlich nichts besonderes.Die Saison ist vorbei. Wie geht es bei Ihnen?

Mit freundl.Gruessen,

Ihr,

A card from Johannes Kleiman to Erich Elias, Otto's brother-in-law in Switzerland. He uses veiled language to let him know that eve 'yore is doing well.

During the hiding period Johannes Kleiman corresponds with Otto Frank's mother in Basel, Switzerland. On 21 August 1942 he congratulates her on the birthday of her daughter-in-law Lotti. Her birthday, however, is on 26 January. Stamps show the card has been meticulously checked by German censorship.

/ 105

After the war, Miep Gies finds this shopping list in the pocket of her coat. Hermann van Pels has written down a few things for her to pick up from the butcher.

On the back of the shopping list Miep has jotted down a cake recipe.

outing never takes place because it's too risky. And Otto Frank doesn't expect the war to last much longer, for the Allies have landed on Sicily.

Anne misses her girlfriends, whom she hasn't seen or spoken to in such a long time. When she thinks about her school friend Hannah Goslar, she realises that she didn't always do her best to understand her. How is Hannah doing? Anne feels a little guilty and powerless. 'If only I could rescue you from wherever you are now, if only I could share with you everything I'm enjoying. But it's too late. I can't help anymore and I can't correct the bad things I've done. But I will never forget her and I will always pray for her!' **/**

27 November 1943

In 1943 the Annexe inhabitants celebrate the Dutch feast of Sinterklaas together for the second time. Anne and her father have written funny poems and come up with small presents for everyone. They all have a good laugh searching for their own shoes in a big basket, with a poem and a present in each shoe. Anne's poem is about her fear of airplanes and anti-aircraft guns, and her present is a sedative pill.

When Christmas comes, Anne writes a short story entitled 'Movie Star Illusion'. The inspiration for the story is Mrs van Pels, who keeps asking her if she wants to be a movie star when she grows up. Anne is crazy about movies, and she reads everything about them that she can get her hands on. Helper Bep Voskuijl often goes to the movies with her fiancé and then gives the Annexe inhabitants a full report. Usually Anne has read the reviews by then and can provide a blow-by-blow description. She's pasted photos of famous movie stars all over the walls of her room.

In the story 'Movie Star Illusion', the main character, Anne Franklin (!), goes to Hollywood at the invitation of Priscilla Lane. The sisters Priscilla, Rosemary, and Lola Lane were actual movie stars. Anne gets acquainted with them and stays with the family. At Priscilla's suggestion, Anne auditions for a tennis racket manufacturer and gets the part! But after a couple of tiring days of shooting she's had enough. She's exhausted from all the costume changes, smiling, and makeup. With Mother Lane's help she's able to quit. Anne Franklin is 'forever cured of her illusion of celebrity'. / So Anne says goodbye to her dream of becoming a movie star, but the idea of becoming famous does appeal to her.

Anne Frank,
Verhalen rondom het achterhuis,
1960

8

CONSOLATION

The Frank family is Jewish, but neither Otto nor
Edith were raised as orthodox believers. The
Franks do not follow the Jewish dietary laws, for
example. When the Frank family lives on the
Merwedeplein in Amsterdam, Edith and Margot
regularly attend services at the liberal Jewish
synagogue. Otto and Anne go with them once or
twice.

After school, Anne and Margot have lessons
with Rabbi Mehler, the liberal Jewish rabbi, who
teaches them about the history of the Jewish
people, among other things. In November 1940
Anne writes to her grandma in Switzerland,
'Jewish lessons have been cancelled for the time
being, and when the winter comes I don't think I
can go either, because then I'll have to come
home in the dark, and I'd rather not do that, and
I'm not allowed to.'

The first time Anne writes about God in her
diary is when her mother gives her a prayer book
to read. The book does not go down well. 'I read
some prayers in German, just to be good. They
sound nice but they don't mean much to me. Why
is she making me act so pious all of a sudden?' *

Anne doesn't care very much about Jewish rituals in the Secret Annexe either. After the war, Otto Frank recalls that 'Anne never showed any particular interest when we celebrated Jewish holidays, or when Mr Pfeffer said his Friday evening prayers. She just stood quietly by.' *I*

Anne Frank House, *Anne's World*, 2010

Hanukkah is the only Jewish holiday that Anne writes about in her diary. It's December 1942. 'We didn't make much of a fuss about Hanukkah, just gave each other a few nice presents and then the candles. We only kept them lit for 10 minutes because there's a candle shortage, but as long as we don't skip the song it's fine.' *I* Anne's first celebration of Sinterklaas is one day later, and she enjoys it much more.

7 December 1942

The next year, 1943, Hanukkah is celebrated with tasty treats. Anne reports that Hermann and Auguste van Pels gave spice cookies to Margot, Anne, and Peter, and that Fritz Pfeffer asked Miep to bake a cake for Auguste van Pels and Edith Frank.

According to Otto Frank, Fritz Pfeffer is the only one of the Annexe inhabitants who is genuinely religious. In one of her short stories Anne describes Fritz Pfeffer at prayer. She's always relieved when he's done because his praying makes her quite nervous. Anne herself always prays in the evenings with her father.

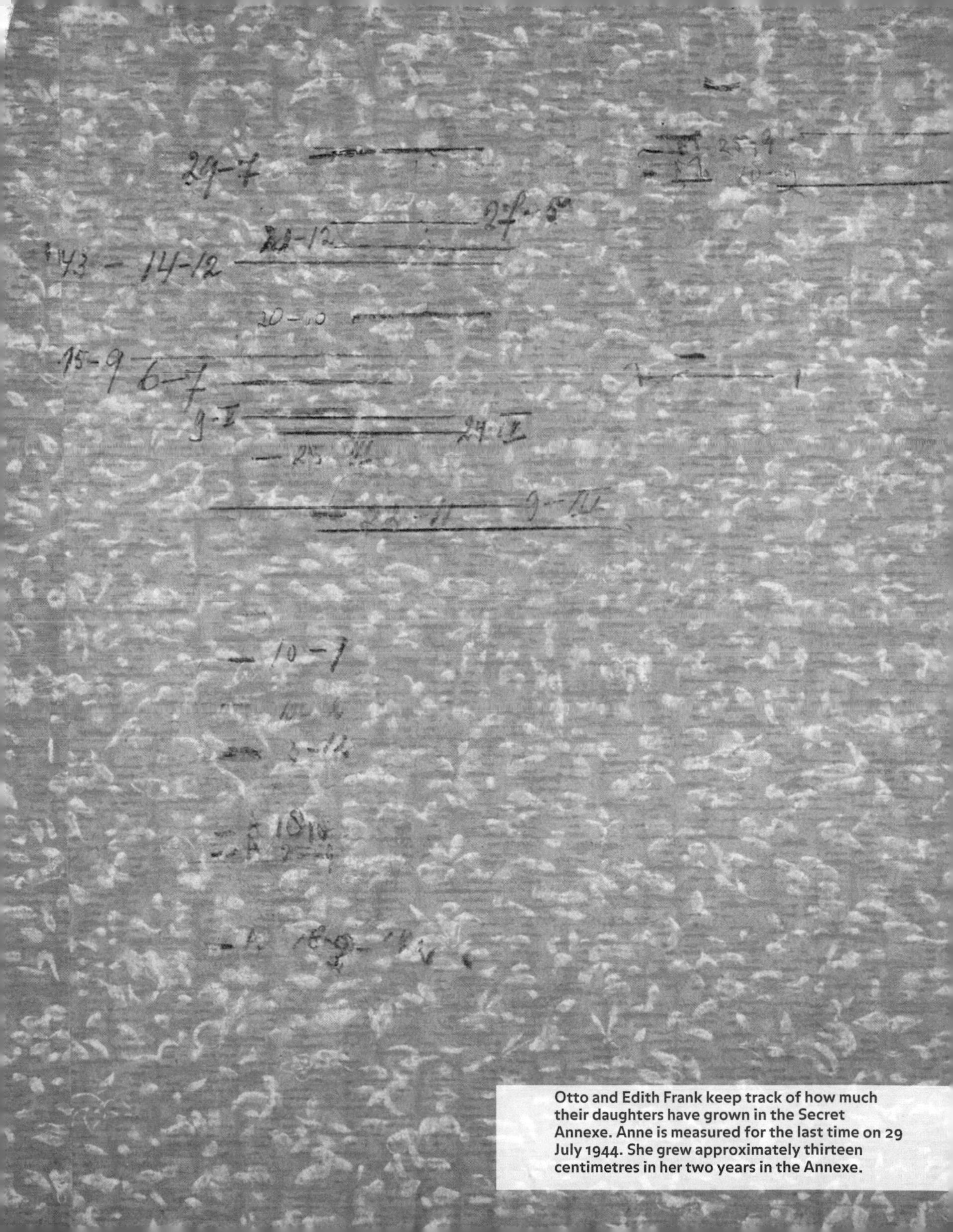

29-7

27-5°

143 - 14-12   23-12

20-10

15-9 6-7

9-II   27-IV

25.VII

22-11   9-III

10-7

3-11

18

Otto and Edith Frank keep track of how much their daughters have grown in the Secret Annexe. Anne is measured for the last time on 29 July 1944. She grew approximately thirteen centimetres in her two years in the Annexe.

The temporarily refurnished room of Otto, Edith, and Margot Frank, 1998.

Edith Frank, May 1935.

Otto Frank, 1936.

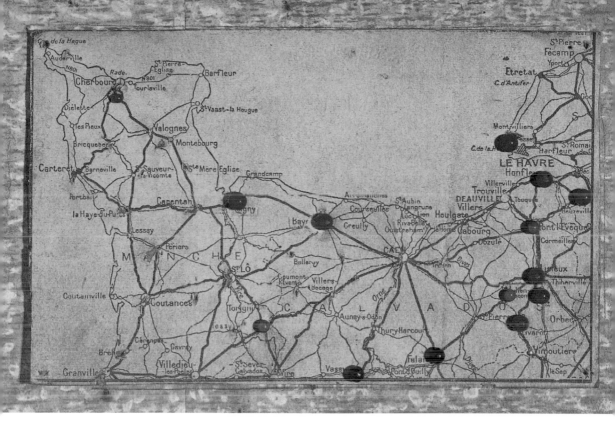

After the landing of the Allies in France on 6 June 1944, the Annexe inhabitants keep track of the advance on this map, using pins.

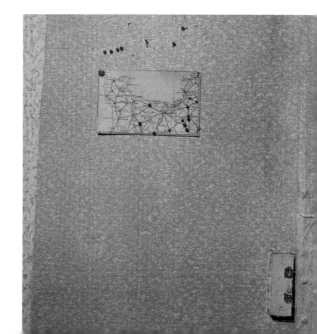

The map of Normandy, photographed in 1954.

Margot Frank, early forties.

The lavatory in the Secret Annexe. Flushing the toilet as little as possible during the day was one of the safety regulations in the Secret Annexe.

In the evening the Annexe inhabitants can wash themselves in this bathroom. A strict schedule is drawn up for this purpose. Anne has from eight thirty to nine thirty to give herself a thorough washing.

The storage area on the second floor of the front part of the building is temporarily refurnished, 1998.

The storage area on the second floor, 1954.

Bep Voskuijl, Miep Gies, Esther, and Pine Wuurman in front of 263 Prinsengracht, May 1941.

The warehouse, 1998.

The front of 263 Prinsengracht, late fifties.

From Anne's diary we learn that she did come to know God. The texts that she copies out in her 'beautiful sentences book' in the second half of 1943 are often religious in nature. Anne is very concerned about the fate of the Jews. She prays that God will spare them and is grateful for all the good things He has given her.

Anne's religious sensibility gives her consolation and connects her with nature. Before going into hiding Anne wasn't much interested in nature, but now that she's been forced to stay indoors for so long she realises what she's missing: 'When I sat at the window this morning (...) and looked outside and actually took a long, deep look at God and nature, it made me happy, nothing but happy.' *I* Anne is convinced of the power of nature, because God is there: 'For anyone who is frightened, lonely, or unhappy, the very best remedy is to go outside, to a place where you can be completely alone, alone with the sky, nature, and God. Because only then can you feel that everything is as it should be and that God wants to see people happy in the simple beauty of nature.' *I*

Although anxiety is a constant presence in Anne's life, she gradually finds more courage with the help of God. She also believes her life has been improved by her friendship with Peter. 'God has not left me on my own nor will He leave me alone.' *I*

23 February 1944

17 February 1944

31 March 1944

9
'Friends are on the way'

/ 6 June 1944

January 1944 —
3 August 1944

At the end of January 1944, Anne leafs through her diary. She realises that she has a deep hunger for trust, love, and physical affection. Not long afterwards Anne has an extraordinary dream. She dreams about Peter Schiff, a boy who lived in her neighbourhood and who she had a huge crush on. When she was eleven and he was thirteen they hung around together all summer long, until Peter moved. After that he cut off all contact with her. Anne thought he found her too childish and decided it made no sense to pursue him. But she couldn't get him out of her mind. In Anne's dream Peter says to her, 'If I had known that, I would have come to you long ago ...!' **/** She feels his cheek **6 January 1944** against hers and they look deep into each other's eyes. Anne is very happy with her dream because it makes her feel as if her great love is somehow still with her. It makes her feel less alone.

In one of Anne's short stories, the protagonist, Anne Franklin, goes to visit the Hollywood stars Priscilla and Rosemary Lane.

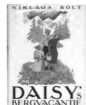

A selection of the books that Anne mentions in
her diary.

Alice Bretz

HET LIED DER
DUISTERNIS

In her 'beautiful sentences book' Anne copies
out a long passage from the Dutch translation of
the book *I Begin Again* by Alice Bretz.

/ 134

Otto and Edith Frank make sure there are plenty
of schoolbooks in the Annexe so Margot and
Anne don't fall too far behind.

Anne Frank.

HERDRUKKEN EN NIEUWE UITGAVEN

A. L. VAN HULZEN, **Leesstof.** Bloemlezing uit onze beste schrijvers voor de Hogere Klassen van het Middelbaar- en Voorbereidend Hoger Onderwijs en het Kweekschoolonderwijs, gebonden . . . . f 1.50

HORN en DE GAST, **Beginselen der Plantkunde,** ten dienste van de Lagere Klassen van het Middelbaar- en Voorbereidend Hoger Onderwijs, 10e druk, geheel herzien door F. C. CAMMEL, Leraar H.B.S. 5-j. cursus te Rotterdam, met 256 figuren in de tekst en 2 driekleurendrukplaten . f 1.50 gebonden . . . . f 1.75

S. W. F. MARGADANT, **Lexilogus.** Latijnse en Griekse werkwoorden met compositia en andere afleidingen, voorzien van aantekeningen omtrent betekenis en etymologie. Een aanvulling op grammatica en woordenboek voor gymnasiasten en hen, die zich tot het Staatsexamen voorbereiden, f 1.—, gebonden . . . . f 1.50

Dr. S. WARTENA, Ovidius Naso, Tristia, I. Tekst. II. Aantekeningen, samen . . . . f 1.25

R. A. OVERDIEP en H. TURKSTRA, **Het Nieuwe Admissie-Examen** voor Middelbare Scholen en Gymnasia. Een keuze uit de Rekenopgaven van meer dan 100 toelatingsexamens, methodisch gerangschikt en bewerkt, 2e druk, met Antwoorden . . . . f 0.60

Dr. D. P. A. VERRIJP, **Leerboek der Goniometrie en Vlakke Trigonometrie,** met omstreeks 1150 opgaven, 4e druk, met Formules op afzonderlijk karton . . . . . . f 1.75 gebonden . . . . f 2.—

—.—, Inleiding tot de Goniometrie, voor Begin-onderwijs op Gymnasia, H.B.S. A, etc. . . . . . . f 0.25

—.—, Sphérische Trigonometrie, met 200 opgaven . . f 0.25

—.—, Determinanten, bestemd voor beginners . . . . f 0.25

N.V. JOH. YKEMA'S UITGEVERS-MAATSCHAPPIJ 'S-GRAVENHAGE

Augustus 1941.
achterhuis.

FRANS

VOOR HET MIDDELBAAR- EN VOORBEREIDEND HOGER ONDERWIJS

DOOR

H. J. SCHOO EN A. H. VAN DER WEEL

II

HULPBOEKJE

TWEEDE DRUK

1940

N.V. JOH. YKEMA'S UITGEVERS-MIJ 'S-GRAVENHAGE

TAKKEN IN HET VOORJAAR.
Links: Elzetakken. *Boven:* Wilgetakken. *Rechts:* Hazelaar.

115

Opmerking. Indien een boom ontstaat uit een stek en niet uit een zaad, ontwikkelen zich alleen een aantal *bijworteis,* die zich vertakken en eveneens houtachtig worden.

1. **De hazelaar** (Córylus Avellána). (Pl. II en fig. 122.) Lang voor de bladeren te voorschijn komen, openbaart het nieuwe leven van de hazelaar zich, in de lange gele katjes, die wolken van stuifmeel kunnen ontlasten.

Aan zo'n hazelaartak kan men waarnemen:
a. een aantal *katjes* (2);
b. een aantal *knoppen,* waarvan de dikste-aan hun top een bundeltje *donkerrode draadjes* dragen (4).

De katjes zijn niet alle even lang. De kortere zijn stevig en ineengedrongen. De langere zijn slap en beweeglijk en geven, vooral in de zon, veel stuifmeel af.

Een *katje* is als volgt gebouwd: Langs de hoofd-as staan een groot aantal ongesteelde bloempjes, elk in de oksel van een schutblad. Elk bloempje bestaat *alleen uit meeldraden;* vier verdubbelde,

Fig. 122. *Hazelaar.*
1. Takje met jonge katjes en knoppen, benevens een blad. 2. Takje met één vrouwelijke en twee mannelijke katjes. 3. Een meeldraadbloempje van onderen gezien. 4. Van terzijde. 5. Een verdubbelde meeldraad. 6. Een stamperkatje. 7. Een stamperbloem. 8. Vrucht met huls 9. Noot. (Uit: Warburg.)

terwijl alle overige bloemdelen ontbreken (3 en 4). Zulk een bloempje heet *onvolkomen.* Wanneer een aantal bloemen ongesteeld langs een niet vertakte hoofdas zit, heet de bloeiwijze, die zo ontstaat, een *aar.* Zijn bovendien de bloemen uitsluitend ééuslachtig, dan heet de aar een *katje.* Een *katje is dus een aartje van éénslachtige bloemen.* We spreken dus van

---

A page from Anne's botany textbook.

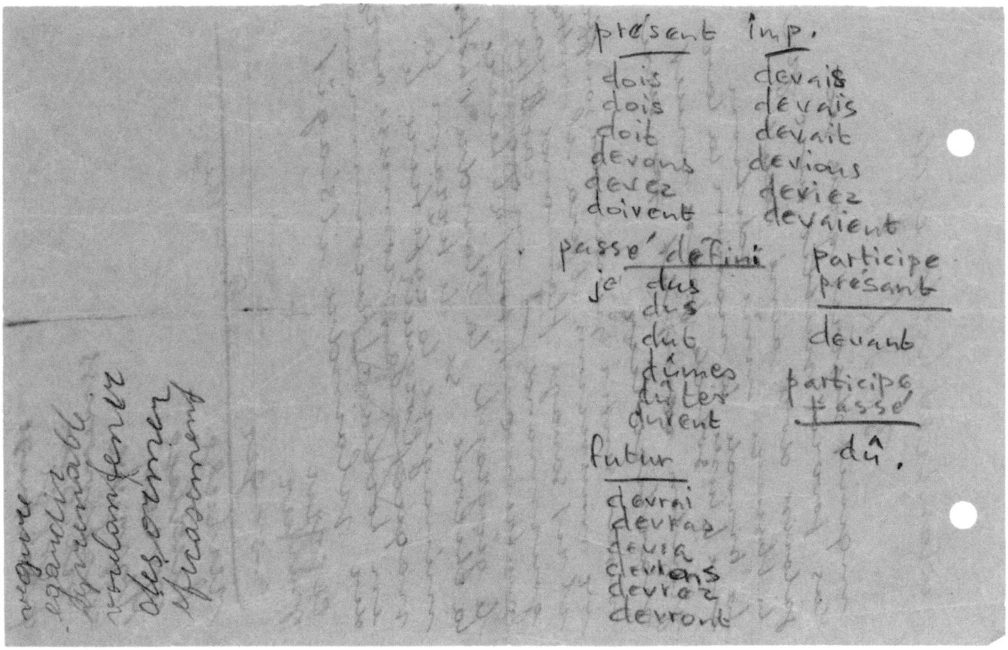

présent   **imp.**

dois   devais
dois   devais
doit   devait
devons   devions
devez   deviez
doivent   devaient

passé défini   **participe**
je dus   **présent**
dus
dut   devant
dûmes
dûtes   **participe**
durent   **passé**

futur   dû.

devrai
devras
devra
devrons
devrez
devront

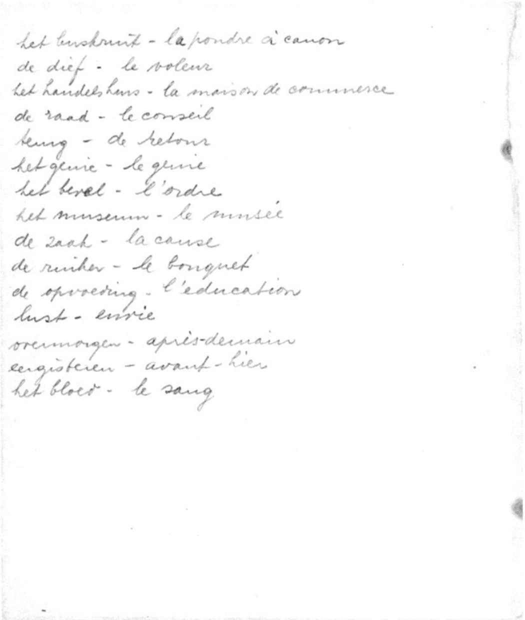

het buskruit - la poudre à canon
de dief - le voleur
het handelshuis - la maison de commerce
de raad - le conseil
terug - de retour
het genie - le génie
het bevel - l'ordre
het museum - le musée
de zaak - la cause
de ruiker - le bouquet
de opvoeding - l'éducation
lust - envie
overmorgen - après-demain
eergisteren - avant-hier
het bloed - le sang

Anne's page of conjugations of the French verb
devoir (must), as well as a page with French words.

to help when she had problems? Do they really deserve such a scathing letter? Anne is deeply shaken by the talk. She regrets what she wrote, and finally she admits that her father is right. 'It's a good thing I've been brought back down to earth and my pride has taken a few knocks, because I was much too satisfied with myself.' *

7 May 1944

A few weeks later Anne's thoughts are dominated by another subject. On 28 March 1944, Minister Bolkestein made an announcement from London on Radio Oranje, the station of the Dutch government in exile. He asked the Dutch people to save their diaries and other documents, such as letters, so that when the war is over it will be possible to investigate what happened in the Netherlands during the German occupation. Anne is inspired by this announcement. She seriously begins thinking about writing a book about her time in the Secret Annexe. 'In any case, after the war I want to publish a book entitled "The Secret Annexe". Whether I'll succeed or not remains to be seen, but I'll base it on my diary.' *

11 May 1944

On 6 June 1944 there's fantastic news on the radio: Allied troops have landed in occupied France with the aim of liberating Europe from the Nazis. The inhabitants and their helpers are beside themselves: is an end finally coming to the war and their difficult time in the Secret Annexe? 'Oh, Kitty, the best thing about the

'No Jews allowed'. The beach in Zandvoort,
spring of 1941.

Starting in September 1941 these wooden signs
are seen hanging all over Amsterdam.

A flower market in Utrecht, 1942. The girl in the foreground is wearing a Star of David.

A cafe on Utrechtsestraat in Amsterdam, 1942. In the window is a sign that says 'No Jews allowed'. A Jewish couple is standing in front of the window.

On 25 May 1943, seven thousand Jews are told to report for transport to Westerbork. Only five hundred of them obey.

One month later, on 20 June 1943, a large roundup takes place in Amsterdam. More than five thousand Jews are arrested and taken to Westerbork transit camp.

A group of arrested Jews in Amsterdam,
20 June 1943.

Jewish children in hiding in the countryside, 1943.

Members of the resistance find hiding places with farmers for a large number of Jewish children.

A person hiding under the roof of a garage.

A woman shows off a hiding place in the crawl
space of a tobacco company in the heart of
Amsterdam shortly after the war.

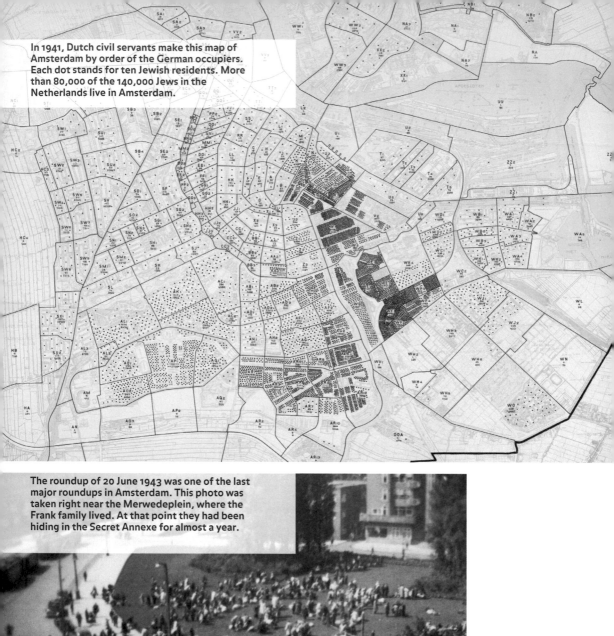

In 1941, Dutch civil servants make this map of Amsterdam by order of the German occupiers. Each dot stands for ten Jewish residents. More than 80,000 of the 140,000 Jews in the Netherlands live in Amsterdam.

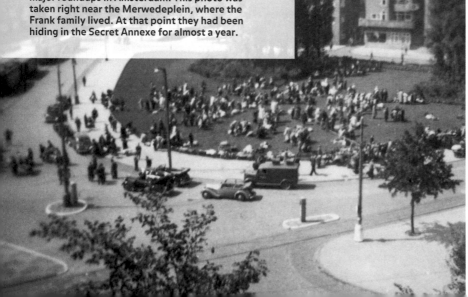

The roundup of 20 June 1943 was one of the last major roundups in Amsterdam. This photo was taken right near the Merwedeplein, where the Frank family lived. At that point they had been hiding in the Secret Annexe for almost a year.

10

HAPPINESS

It's in the Secret Annexe that Anne discovers her talent. The little girl of thirteen who dreamt of a career as a Hollywood movie star has changed into a passionate writer. 'I want to keep on living after my death! And that's why I'm so grateful to God that even at my birth He gave me a chance to develop into a writer, so I can give voice to everything inside me!' /

25 March 1944

For Anne, writing is the one way to open up her heart. 'I still think the most wonderful thing of all is that at least I can write down what I think and feel. Otherwise I'd suffocate completely.' / In her diary letters to Kitty she can get everything off her chest, her most intimate feelings and thoughts. 'Because I came here when I was barely 13 years old, I got a head start thinking and learning about myself, that I'm a person in my own right.' /

16 March 1944

6 January 1944

Anne undergoes a profound change in the Secret Annexe. She becomes an adult. She's surrounded by adults, she's an avid reader, she writes short stories, and she rewrites her diary. She even starts writing a novel entitled *Cady's Life*. Yet after a while she decides she's still too at gunpoint by a policeman in uniform: SS-Oberscharführer Karl Josef Silberbauer. He is clearly in charge.

'Where are your valuables?' he snarls in German. He picks up a briefcase and shakes out the contents. It's Otto's briefcase, where Anne has kept her diaries, notebooks, and other notations. Everything falls on the floor. The Annexe inhabitants turn over their jewellery and their money.

'Get Ready. All of you back here in five minutes.' While the inhabitants gather together the clothing and other items they think they'll be needing, Silberbauer's eye falls on Otto Frank's grey military box, which has 'Leutnant d. Res. Otto Frank' written on it. Otto fought in the German army during the First World War. Surprised, Silberbauer asks Otto, 'Where did you get this chest?' 'It is my own.' 'How did you get it?' 'I was an officer in the First War.' For a moment Silberbauer is at a loss for words. Then he asks, 'Then why didn't you report your status?' 'Why, man, you would have been treated decently! You would have been sent to Theresienstadt.' [a concentration camp]...' Otto doesn't respond. 'Take it easy then...' / says Silberbauer, his tone less harsh.

Ernst Schnabel, *Footsteps of Anne Frank*, 2015

Otto Frank tells him they've been living in the hiding place for more than two years.

19

„Je hebben toch afgesproken dat we geen ruzie zouden maken, ik ben van plan me daaraan te houden!"
„Ik ook Peter, maar vader dacht het niet van ons,
hij dacht dat we kameraden waren, vind jij dat
dat we niet kan?"
„Ik wel en jij?"
„Ik ook. Ik heb ook tegen vader gezegd, dat ik je
vertrouw. Ik vertrouw op je, Peter, net zo vol-
komen als ik het op vader doe en ik geloof dat
je dat waard bent, is 't niet?"
„Ik hoop het (Hij was erg verlegen en rood altijd)
„Ik geloof in je Peter," vervolgde ik, „ik geloof dat
je een goed karakter hebt en dat je vooruit
zult komen in de wereld."
We spraken daarna over andere dingen, later zei
ik nog: „Als we hieruit komen, weet ik wel
dat je je om mij niet meer zult bekommeren!"
Hij raakte in vuur, „dat is niet waar Anne, o nee,
dat mag je niet van me denken!"
Toen werden we geroepen.

Vader sprak met hem, hij vertelde het mij Maandag. „Je vader dacht dat die kameraadschap
wel eens in verliefdheid uit kon lopen," zei hij,

This is the last volume of Anne's diary. It covers the period from 17 April 1944 to 1 August 1944. These diary pages were written on 2 May 1944.

dan nodig is. De man is in zulke dingen altijd de actieve, de vrouw kan tegenhouden.
Het is buiten als je vrij bent heel iets anders,
je ziet andere jongens en meisjes, je kan eens
weg gaan, sport doen en van alles, maar
hier, als je hier teveel samen zit en je wilt
weg kun je niet, je ziet elkaar elk uur,
altijd eigenlijk. Wees voorzichtig Anne, en vat
het niet te ernstig op!"
„Dat doe ik niet vader, maar Peter is fat-
soenlijk, hij is een lieve jongen!"
„Ja, maar hij heeft geen sterk karakter, hij
is licht naar de goede, maar ook licht
naar de slechte kant te beïnvloeden, ik hoop
voor hem dat hij goed blijft, want in zijn
aard is hij goed!"
We praatten nog wat door en spraken af, dat
vader ook met hem zou praten.
Zondagmiddag op de voorzolder vroeg hij: „En
heb je met je vader gesproken, Anne?"
„Ja," antwoordde ik, „ik zal het je wel ver-
tellen. Vader vindt het niet erg, maar hij
zegt dat er hier, waar we zo op elkaar zitten
licht botsingen kunnen komen."

Open >

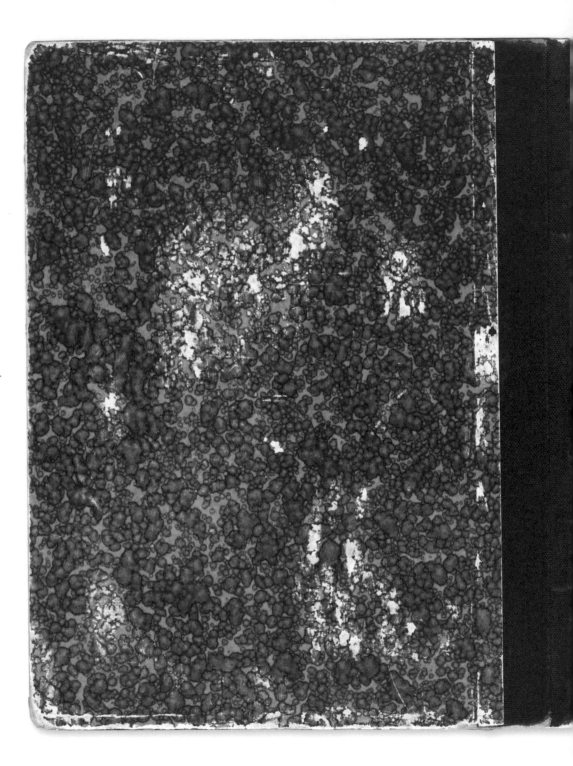

Lieve Vader,   5 Mei 1944.

Omdat ik geloof dat je een verklaring van mij verwacht zal ik je die geven en omdat ik beter schrijven dan spreken kan, doe ik het op papier

Ik denk dat je je in mij teleurgesteld voelt, dat je meer terughouding van mij ver-wacht hebt en daarom zit je te piekeren over dingen die geen gepraten nodig hebben. Van af dat wij hier zijn in Juli 1942 tot een paar weken geleden heb ik het heus niet makkelijk gehad. Als je eens wist wat ik 's avonds niet al uitgehuild heb, hoe wan-hopig en ongelukkig ik was, hoe eenzaam ik me voelde, als je dat eens wist dan zou je wel kunnen begrijpen dat ik naar boven wel! Ik heb het niet van de ene op de andere dag klaargespeeld, om zover te komen, dat ik helemaal zonder moeder en zonder steun van wie dan ook kan leven; het heeft me veel, heel veel strijd en tranen gekost om zo zelf-standig te worden als ik nu ben.

Moeder kan lachen en jij kunt me niet ge-loven, het kan me niets schelen, ik weet dat

On 5 May 1944 Anne writes an angry letter to her father. He says he's going to burn the letter, but in the end he saves it.

ik een mens alleen ben en ik voel me door
niets verantwoordelijk tegenover jullie.
Ik heb je dit alleen verteld, omdat ik dacht
dat je me anders te stiekum zou vinden*,
maar je hoeft niet te denken dat ik daar-
mee de verantwoordelijkheid van me af-
geschoven heb verantwoording voor mijn
daden heb ik alleen aan me zelf af te
leggen, daar heeft geen vader en geen moeder
recht op!
Toen ik in moeilijkheden zat hebben jullie en
ook jij je ogen dichtgedaan en je oren dicht-
gestopt, je hebt me niet geholpen, integendeel, niets dan standjes voor mijn lichtzin-
tigheid heb ik gekregen. Ik was lichtzinnig
alleen om niet aldoor tobberig te zijn, ik
was overmoedig om niet steeds die stem van
binnen te horen. Ik heb comedie gespeeld,
anderhalf jaar lang, dag in, dag uit,
ik ben niet uit m'n rol gevallen, heb
niet geblaasd en heb nergens iemand
gehad die zich iets van me aantrok, niets
van dat alles, en toch heb ik overwonnen,
want ik ben uitgestreden!
* omdat ik je beloofd mede, omdat ik dacht
dat jij het dadelijk zou begrijpen

Ik ben zelfstandig naar lichaam en geest,
ik heb geen moeder meer nodig, ik ben door
al die strijd sterk geworden!
En nu, nu ik er bovenop ben, nu ik weet
dat ik uitgevochten heb, nu wil ik ook zelf
m'n weg verder gaan, de weg die ik goed
vind. Je kunt en mag me niet als 14
beschouwen, ik ben door alle moeilijkheid
ouder geworden. Ik zal geen spijt over m'n
daden hebben, ik zal handelen zoals ik
denk dat ik dat kan doen, en ik weet
heel goed wat ik doen kan.
Je kunt me niet zachtzinnig van boven
weghouden, óf je verbiedt me alles, óf je
vertrouwt me door dik en door dun.
En ik vraag dat laatste van je, hoewel je
misschien het niet graag zult doen, laat
me alleen, als je niet voor altijd m'n
vertrouwen wilt verliezen!
                    Je kind;

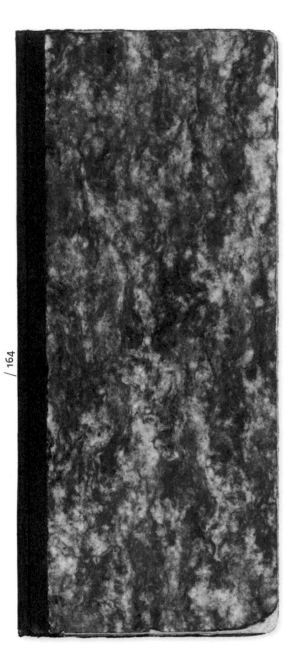

In June 1943 Anne starts her 'beautiful sentences book'. Anne copies out short and long passages from books she reads in the Secret Annexe.

Cover and contents page of Anne's story book.

On 20 May 1944 Anne starts working on her novel
about her time in the Secret Annexe.

Anne's diaries and her rewritten version
on loose pages.

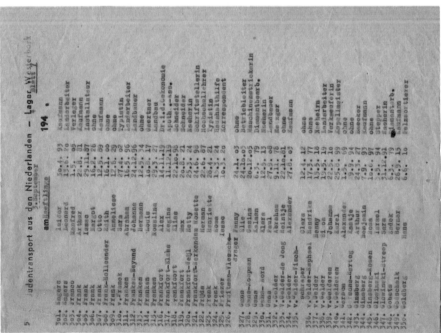

Included on these pages of the list of prisoners being transported on 3 September 1944 are the names of the Frank family, the Van Pels family, and Fritz Pfeffer.

Bram Asscher is also a prisoner in Westerbork. On 25 August 1944 he writes to his mother and his Uncle Dik, 'Mama, did you know that Margot is here? That friend of Trees. You remember her, don't you? She's in the punishment barracks with her parents and her sister. Terrible!'

Nur die Linien beschreiben!

Nur die Linien beschreiben!

Antwort-Briefkarten anbei.

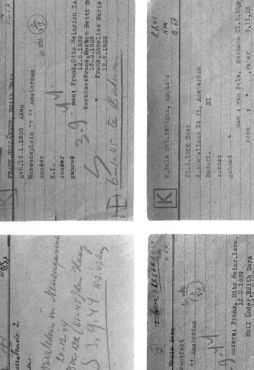

The identity cards of the eight Secret Annexe inhabitants from the records of the Jewish Council in Amsterdam. After the war the Red Cross uses these cards to trace the fate of deported Jews. Otto's identity card notes: 'Returned!'.

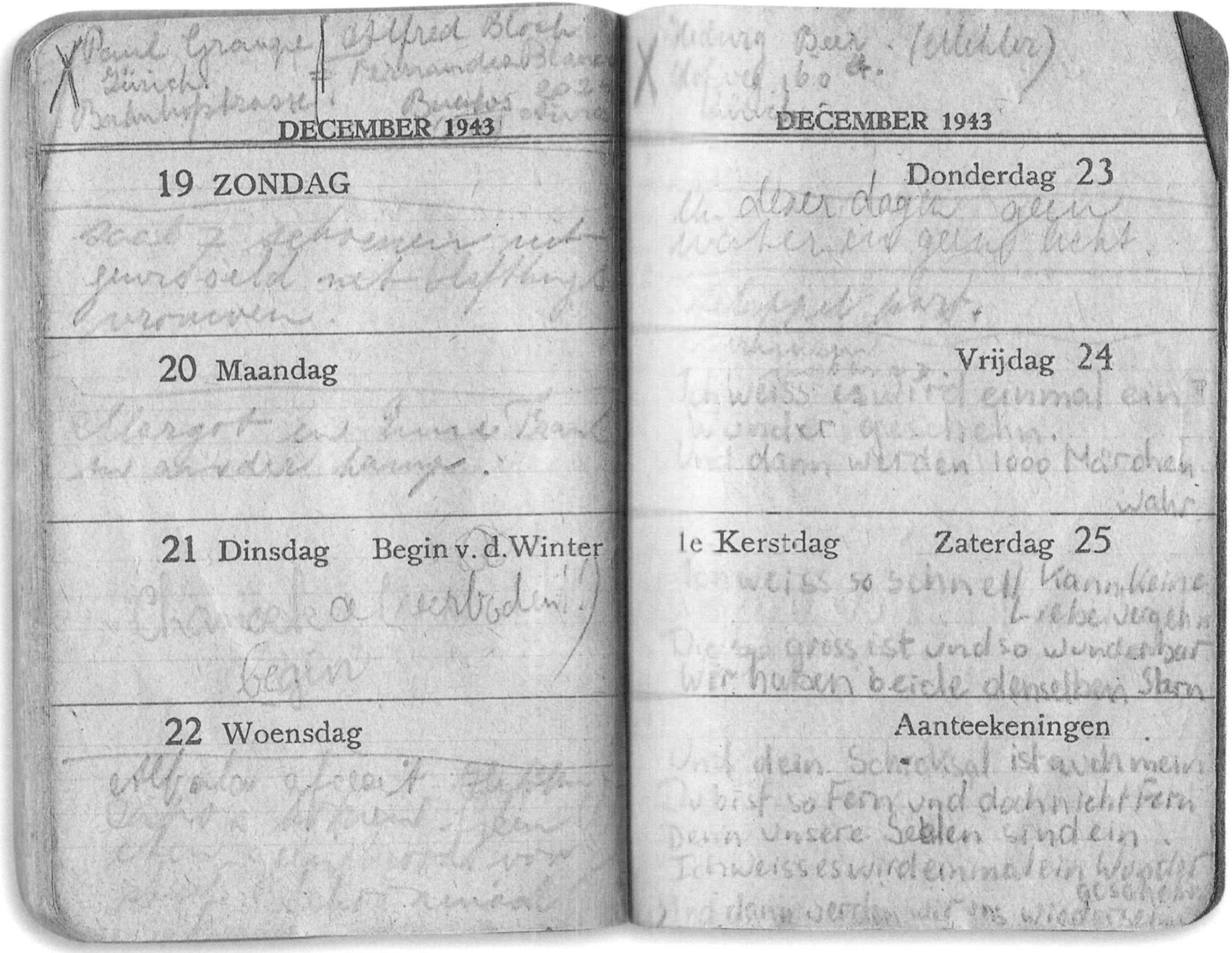

The date book belonging to Ruth Wiener, from Bergen-Belsen concentration camp. Like Hannah Goslar she is a prisoner in the Sternlager, another part of the camp. It's a date book for the year 1943, but Ruth also uses it for 1944 and 1945. On 20 December 1944 she notes, 'Margot and Anne Frank in other camp.'

DECEMBER 1943

19 ZONDAG

20 Maandag

21 Dinsdag Begin v. d. Winter

22 Woensdag

DECEMBER 1943

Donderdag 23

Vrijdag 24

Zaterdag 25 1e Kerstdag

Aanteekeningen

Once again Silberbauer is surprised. To prove the truth of this statement, Otto asks Anne to stand in front of the lines that have been marked on the wallpaper indicating how many centimetres she has grown in all that time. Silberbauer is forced to believe him.

Once the inhabitants have gathered everything they can take with them, they are told to wait in the director's room. Kugler and Kleiman join them. When Silberbauer attempts to interrogate the two helpers, they both say they have nothing to report. 'All right, then you'll come along too.' **/** The helpers Miep Gies and Bep Voskuijl are left alone. In the meantime, one of the policemen has called for a larger car, since they hadn't counted on arresting ten people.

For the first time, after having been locked up in the Secret Annexe for more than two years, Anne is outside. But there's a sealed truck parked at the door. One by one, the eight Annexe inhabitants and two helpers get in. The truck goes to the office of the Sicherheitsdienst, the German police, where they're all interrogated. After one night at the Sicherheitsdienst, the inhabitants are taken to the house of detention on the Weteringschans and the two helpers to the house of detention on the Amstelveenseweg.

Early on Tuesday morning, 8 August, the Annexe inhabitants are told to get ready for

Ernst Schnabel,
*Footsteps of
Anne Frank,*
2015

transport. They're taken to Amsterdam's Central Station along with about eighty other prisoners. All of them are sent by train to the Westerbork transit camp in the province of Drente.

'We travelled in a regular passenger train. The fact that the door was bolted did not matter very much to us. (...) Anne would not move from the window. Outside, it was summer. Meadows, stubble fields, and villages flew by. The telephone wires along the right of way curvetted up and down along the windows. It was like freedom.'
 Otto Frank *

Ernst Schnabel, *Footsteps of Anne Frank*, 2015

After more than four hours the Annexe inhabitants arrive in Westerbork. They're registered and imprisoned in a punishment barracks. The punishment barracks – where one section is for men and another for women – are where all the Jews who did not report voluntarily are kept. The punishment barracks are in a different part of the camp and are fenced off by barbed wire.

The prisoners in these barracks are handled more strictly than the others. They have to turn in their clothing and to wear blue overalls with red shoulder pieces. Sewn on the overalls is a yellow star bearing the word 'Jew'. They are given wooden shoes instead of ordinary shoes.

The men's heads are shaved and they have to wear caps.

These 'punishment cases', such as the inhabitants of the Secret Annexe, have to get up at five-thirty in the morning and are then taken to work by the 'Ordedienst', prisoners who serve as guards.

Anne, Margot, their mother, and Auguste van Pels are sent to a large work barracks with other prisoners, where they break up old batteries and put the components in separate baskets. It's filthy work. The batteries contain carbon bars that give off a black deposit, which covers their hands and faces. It's also very dusty in the barracks.

Every day they work from seven to twelve o'clock with a twenty-minute break. At twelve o'clock the prisoners, accompanied by the 'Ordedienst', are taken back to the residential barracks to eat. At one-thirty they return to the work barracks, where they work straight through from two to seven o'clock, with another twenty-minute break. At seven their long work day is over.

'We all had to work in the camp, but we had the evenings free to spend with each other. It was something of a relief, especially for the children, not to be locked up anymore and to be able to talk to other people. But we elders were afraid of being deported to the infamous camps in [Nazi-occupied] Poland.'

Otto Frank /

Anne Frank House, www.annefrank.org, 2016

After a meagre cold meal the prisoners have their evenings to themselves. On Sunday the 'punishment cases' have to get up at five o'clock. The men do compulsory exercising from a quarter to six until eight o'clock, while the women do gymnastics during the same period. The rest of Sunday is 'free'.

Rosa de Winter-Levy, her husband, and her daughter Judy are prisoners in Westerbork along with the Frank family. After the war Rosa recalls: 'I saw Anne Frank and Peter van Daan [Peter van Pels] every day in Westerbork. They were always together (...) In Westerbork Anne was lovely, so radiant that her beauty flowed over into Peter. She was very pallid at first, but there was something so intensely attractive about her frailty and her expressive face that at first Judy was too shy to make friends with her.' /

Ernst Schnabel, *Footsteps of Anne Frank,* 2015

On 2 September the 'Ordedienst' announces that on the following day a thousand prisoners will be put on the train to the east. Included on the long list of names read out that night are those of the Secret Annexe inhabitants, along with almost all the punishment barracks prisoners.

The next morning a long freight train is waiting for them. The punishment prisoners turn in their blue overalls and are given their own clothing in return. Seventy-five prisoners are crammed into each carriage. They have one barrel of drinking water and an empty barrel to serve as a toilet. The Frank family are able to travel together in the same carriage.

After a few hours the train stops, and loaves of bread and a keg of sugar beet jam are thrown into the carriage. Then the train thunders on. Later the train stops again. The doors open and the prisoners are forced to hand over to the guards any valuables they still may have with them. The water in the carriage runs out. Everyone is thirsty and exhausted. Only on the third night, from 5 to 6 September, does the train reach its destination.

'There are many things I still cannot talk about. There are many things I never want to talk about. Such as my feelings when we were driven from our hiding place in Amsterdam, or on the platform in Auschwitz when my family was broken up and separated.'
Otto Frank /

Welt am Sonntag, 4 February 1979

A transport carrying Jewish prisoners pulls out of
Westerbork, 1943. To the right are members of
the 'Ordedienst'.

A train with prisoners ready to leave Westerbork
transit camp.

A full view of Westerbork transit camp. More than 100,000 Jewish prisoners were transported from this camp to concentration and extermination camps in the east. Only five thousand of them returned.

The sign hanging on the train that travelled back and forth between Westerbork and Auschwitz.

The 'selection' of prisoners on the platform in
Auschwitz-Birkenau, May/June 1944. A woman
with a small child is sent to the gas chamber side.

Jewish women and children on their way to the
gas chamber.

Jewish women with their heads shaved after the 'selection', May/June 1944.

Liberated prisoners in Auschwitz-Birkenau, January 1945.

This part of Bergen-Belsen concentration camp was for female prisoners.

A photo of the Bergen-Belsen camp, April 1945.

Liberated prisoners cook a meal. In the background is a mountain of shoes.

Sick prisoners are given water in one of the barracks, April 1945.

Women and children in one of the barracks, April
1945.

British soldiers force former guards at Bergen-Belsen concentration camp to help bury the bodies.

12

'You could see them dying'

/ Rachel van Amerongen-Frankfoorder in *The Last Seven Months of Anne Frank,* Willy Lindwer, 2004

5/6 September 1944 — February 1945

The carriage doors of the train are shoved open. Bright lights, prisoners in striped suits with clubs in their hands, and guards with dogs in the background. 'Aussteigen, schnell, schneller!' Orders come roaring out of the loudspeakers. 'Leave your luggage behind,' 'Men and women line up separately.' They have arrived at Auschwitz-Birkenau concentration and extermination camp.

Nazi doctors inspect the new prisoners one by one and decide over life and death. Men and women who can work are sent to one side, those who are too old, too sick, or too young to the other. Mothers with children younger than fifteen, as well as pregnant women, must go with the sick and elderly. Of the more than one thousand prisoners who arrive that night, about 350 are immediately murdered in the gas chambers.

12

'You could see
them dying'

/ Rachel van Amerongen-Frankfoorder in *The Last Seven Months of Anne Frank,* Willy Lindwer, 2004

5/6 September 1944 — February 1945

The carriage doors of the train are shoved open. Bright lights, prisoners in striped suits with clubs in their hands, and guards with dogs in the background. 'Aussteigen, schnell, schneller!' Orders come roaring out of the loudspeakers. 'Leave your luggage behind,' 'Men and women line up separately.' They have arrived at Auschwitz-Birkenau concentration and extermination camp.

Nazi doctors inspect the new prisoners one by one and decide over life and death. Men and women who can work are sent to one side, those who are too old, too sick, or too young to the other. Mothers with children younger than fifteen, as well as pregnant women, must go with the sick and elderly. Of the more than one thousand prisoners who arrive that night, about 350 are immediately murdered in the gas chambers.

Edith, Margot, and Anne are sent to the 'work side' along with two hundred other women. They're taken to the bathhouse. There the women are lined up according to the first letter of their last name and wait until they are called in. They must hand in their clothing and stand naked while waiting their turn.

After registration a number is tattooed on their lower arms with a sharp pen. Their heads are shaved and they're sent to the showers. Because there are no more prison uniforms, random dresses and shoes are tossed to them. One gets a light summer dress, another a thick woollen dress. You're lucky to get two shoes that fit.

It's morning by the time the prisoners are lined up and marched in rows of five to their barracks. Every barracks has room for about seven hundred women. There are thousands of women prisoners in the entire Auschwitz-Birkenau women's camp.

The prisoners are put to work. They are made to haul bricks and sods. Every morning, afternoon, and evening there's roll call: the prisoners are forced to line up, regardless of the weather, in order to be counted. They're worked like slaves and given little to eat. Sometimes there's only cabbage soup and a bit of bread. The hygienic conditions are very poor and many fall ill. 'Selections' are held constantly, and the sick are ruthlessly sent to the gas chamber.

Anne and Margot contract scabies, an infectious skin disease, so they're sent to separate barracks. Edith does all she can to scrounge extra food for them. Sometimes she's successful and she's able to pass bread to them through a hole in the barracks wall.

There are also other kinds of 'selections'. At the end of October 1944, the Nazi doctors select prisoners who may be suitable for forced labour in Nazi Germany sometime in the future. Although they're sick and weakened, Margot and Anne are selected, as is Auguste van Pels. Edith Frank is not. She stays behind, in despair.

On 1 November, a freight train with about a thousand selected women pulls out of camp Auschwitz-Birkenau. The women have no idea how long the ride is going to take or what the destination is. Every prisoner is given a chunk of break, a bit of margarine, and a piece of goat cheese for the journey. Each carriage gets a barrel of drinking water.

It's crowded and stuffy with seventy women in a sealed carriage. Soon the food and water run out. Each time an air attack threatens, the train stops and remains stationary until the danger has passed. After a rigorous two-day journey, the train approaches the precincts of Bergen-Belsen concentration camp. The women must cover the last six kilometres on foot. At the camp they are housed in large tents, despite the cold, wet autumn weather.

When the tents collapse a few days later due to a severe storm, the prisoners are sent into the barracks anyway. One day, Auguste van Pels discovers that Anne's school friend Hannah Goslar is also in Bergen-Belsen, in an adjacent part of the camp. She immediately shares the news with Anne.

After more than two years Anne is able to talk to her girlfriend again. Because the two parts of the camp are divided by barbed wire and reeds, they cannot see each other. Hannah is surprised to find Anne here. All this time she thought she was safe in Switzerland. Anne tells her she's in a very bad way. 'We have nothing to eat here, almost nothing, and we're cold, we have no clothes at all, and I'm so skinny, and my head has been shaved.' She believes her father is dead. *I*

In Hannah's part of the camp – the Sternlager – conditions are a bit better. The Nazis are planning on exchanging the prisoners for German prisoners of war. Every now and then they get a food packet from the Red Cross. Hannah gathers a little food for Anne, wraps it up, and tosses it over the fence. But soon she hears Anne screaming loudly: another prisoner

Menno Metselaar, *Anne Frank Magazine*, 1998

has snatched the package and run off with it. They try again later, and this time Anne succeeds in getting the package. The mother of one of Margot's girlfriends is also able to throw a package over the fence. The package contains an old dress, bread, and soap for Anne and Margot.

Margot is already too ill to come to the fence. Like many other prisoners she is suffering from typhus, a contagious disease that is spread by lice. Anne also becomes infected. Rachel van Amerongen-Frankfoorder was a prisoner with Margot and Anne in Bergen-Belsen concentration camp and makes the following report: 'They had those hollowed-out faces, skin over bone. They were terribly cold. They had the least desirable places in the barracks, below, near the door, which was constantly opened and closed. You heard them constantly screaming: "Close the door, close the door," and the voices became weaker every day. You could really see both of them dying, as well as others.' *I*

Margot succombs to the illness in February 1945; Anne dies shortly thereafter.

Willy Lindwer, *The Last Seven Months of Anne Frank,* 2004

Hermann van Pels
1898 – 1944

Hermann van Pels is forced to join a road
construction crew in Auschwitz. It's hard work.
He injures his hand on the job and has to stop
working. After a selection in October 1944
Hermann van Pels is sent to the gas chamber.

Auguste van Pels
1900 – 1945

On 7 February 1945 Auguste van Pels is taken
from Bergen-Belsen to Raguhn, one of the
satellite camps of Buchenwald concentration
camp. On 9 April she is put on a transport to
Thereslenstadt. Auguste van Pels dies on this
transport.

Peter van Pels
1926 – 1945

When Auschwitz is evacuated in January 1945,
Peter van Pels is put on a so-called 'death
march'. After a gruelling journey he arrives at
Mauthausen concentration camp on 25 January.
The heavy forced labour in a Mauthausen
satellite camp takes its toll: Peter dies on 10
May 1945, shortly after the camp is liberated.

Fritz Pfeffer
1889 – 1944

Fritz Pfeffer finally ends up in Neuengamme
concentration camp. There he is put to work at
hard labour. According to the Neuengamme
'death book' Fritz Pfeffer dies on 20 December
1944.

13

'Now I know the whole truth'

/ Otto Frank in a letter to Milly Stanfield, 27 July 1945

January 1945 — 19 August 1980

By the time Margot and Anne Frank succomb to typhus in Bergen-Belsen concentration camp, their father has already been liberated by Russian soldiers. With the Russian army approaching Auschwitz, the camp leaders decide to evacuate. The gas chambers, crematoria, and incriminating documents are destroyed, and all the guards take to their heels. Any prisoners who can still walk are forced to go with them.

Red Cross workers carry the fifteen-year-old Russian prisoner Ivan Dudnik out of the Auschwitz camp, January 1945. He is too weak to walk.

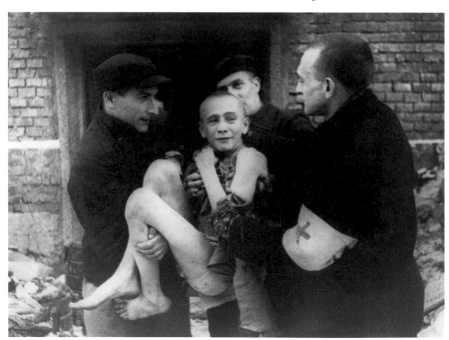

A Russian army doctor
with survivors from
Auschwitz
concentration camp,
January 1945.

Otto Frank is too weak to go and is left
behind in the sick barracks. He is convinced that
the guards are planning on shooting him and
the other remaining prisoners. But because of
the rapid Russian advance, the guards realise
they don't have enough time. On 27 January
1945 the first Russian soldiers enter Auschwitz
concentration camp. There they find about
seven thousand prisoners, many of them more
dead than alive. One of them is Otto Frank. He
weighs only fifty kilos.

For the first weeks after the arrival of the
Russians, Otto stays in the camp. By early
March 1945 he has recovered sufficiently to join
a group of seven hundred liberated Dutch
prisoners who are starting the long journey
back to the Netherlands. He has no idea where
Edith, Margot, and Anne are. He hasn't seen
them since they were separated on the platform
at Auschwitz.

The liberated prisoners have to travel by a
very roundabout route and wait for a long time,
for Nazi Germany has not yet been defeated. In
Katowice, Otto Frank meets Rosa de Winter-Levy.

She has bad news for him concerning Edith, Margot, and Anne. I said to him: 'I know nothing about the children. They were taken away. After a while I told him that his wife had died, in bed, right beside me. Mr Frank did not move when I told him. I looked into his face, but he had turned away, and then he made a movement. I no longer remember exactly what it was, but it seems to me he laid his head on the table.' /

Ernst Schnabel, *Footsteps of Anne Frank,* 2015

This news hits Otto hard, but he hopes that Margot and Anne are still alive. He travels on with the group to Czernowitz and arrives in Odessa at the end of April, where they're put up in a sanatorium near the Black Sea. Suddenly on 8 May they hear the sound of cannon fire: Nazi Germany has capitulated! Great joy! But at the same time there's also concern: what is the situation like in the Netherlands?

Otto Frank and the others wait impatiently for an opportunity to return home. On 21 May a large ship is finally available, the Monowai. Its destination is Marseille in the south of France.

For the passengers, the journey is like a dream after the horrors of Auschwitz. The food on board, the sun on the deck... Otto has the misfortune of having his mattress snatched by one of the passengers, and he has to sleep in a hammock. The ship sails through the Bosphorus to Crete, then through the Strait of Messina to Sardinia and Corsica, and finally arrives in Marseille on the morning of 27 May.

'It was a fantastic reception. There was a band on the quay playing the Wilhelmus and the Marseillaise.' /

Rosa de Winter-Levy, *Aan de gaskamer ontsnapt,* 1945

The Monowai, the ship that Otto Frank takes from Odessa to Marseille.

Party in New York, 7 May 1945. Front page of the *New York World Telegram*.

In June 1945 there are Dutch flags hanging up and down the Kalverstraat, Amsterdam's most famous shopping street.

This 'Carte de Rapatrié' enables Otto Frank to travel from Marseillle to Amsterdam. He has already indicated on the card that he is going to the home of Jan and Miep Gies.

In August 1945 Otto Frank places an advertisement in the newspaper *Het Vrije Volk*. Who can tell him anything about Anne and Margot?

IRMA SPIELMANN, geb. 10-4-'94 Wenen, Tsj. Slow. nation. Weggevoerd Westerborg 23-3-'43. Wie weet iets van dit transport? Spielmann, Scheldestr. 181 III, Zuid.
MARGOT FRANK (19 j.) en ANNA FRANK (16 j.), in Jan. op transp. vanuit Bergen-Belzen. O. Frank, Prinsengracht 263, tel. 37059.
Mijn man ALFRED v. GELDEREN. (Oct. 1942 uit Westerb.) en kinderen DORA ROSA en FREDERIK MARTHIJN (24-7-1942 uit Westerb.) Marianne v. Gelderen—Engelander, Jozef Israëlkade 126 II.
FRANCISCUS JOHANNES MAAS geb. 19-10-'23, werkz. bij Machinefabriek Winger en Co Welters-

The first written statement concerning the death of Margot and Anne in Bergen-Belsen concentration camp. On 11 November 1945, Lien Brilleslijper declares that they 'died in late February or early March [1945]'.

The passengers are registered on site, given medical examinations, and fed a dinner. At seven o'clock in the evening the train leaves for the Netherlands.

The train journey ends in Roermond. Otto has to spend three more days there before he can continue on to Amsterdam, since no trains are running in the Netherlands and there are almost no cars. When he finally arrives in Amsterdam he goes straight to the home of Jan and Miep Gies. Miep notifies Johannes Kleiman and his wife, and Charlotte Kaletta (Fritz Pfeffer's girlfriend). They tell Otto that Bep Voskuijl and Victor Kugler have also survived the war. Otto is overjoyed, because he had been very worried about the helpers. On 4 June he goes to the office on the Prinsengracht for the first time, exactly ten months after the arrest.

Otto Frank moves in with Jan and Miep Gies. On 7 July he writes to his second cousin Milly Stanfield in London: 'I have to accept the fact of Edith's death, but I keep hoping I can find my children. That is what I am living for at the moment. I gravitate between hope and fear.' Otto puts advertisements in the newspapers and goes to Amsterdam Central Station on a regular basis to talk to survivors who arrive there. Have they seen Margot and Anne?

In mid-July Otto meets the sisters Janny and Lien Brilleslijper. They were imprisoned in Bergen-Belsen with Margot and Anne. Janny and Lien tell him about the last months of his daughters' lives. 'Now I know the whole truth,' Otto writes to Milly Stanfield on 27 July. Otto passes on the sad news to Jan and Miep Gies, and Miep in turn gives him the diary, the notebooks, and all of Anne's other writings.

The first newspaper article on the diary of Anne Frank in *Het Parool* of 3 April 1946. *Het Parool* was a resistance newspaper during the war.

Otto Frank in his company's director's office, 1954. He is showing his camp number from Auschwitz: B-9174.

The helpers had found them on the floor after the arrest, and Miep has kept them in a drawer of her desk all this time in the hope of one day being able to return them to Anne.

Otto puts the papers aside for a while. His grief is too great. But when he finally does pick up Anne's diary he can't stop reading it. Otto discovers that he didn't know his daughter Anne very well at all.

'I had no idea of the depth of her thoughts and feelings.' /

Otto Frank, Anne Frank House, www.annefrank.org, 2016

Anne's accurate descriptions of the events in the Secret Annexe bring back many memories of their time in hiding. Otto translates a number of important passages for his family in Switzerland, and he shares parts of the diary with his friends. They think he shouldn't keep the diary to himself, and urge him to have it published. But publication is no simple matter.

One morning, to his great astonishment, Otto Frank reads an article about Anne's diary on the front page of the Amsterdam newspaper *Het Parool*. The historian Jan Romein had been shown the diary by his wife Annie, also an historian. Otto Frank had asked her to help him find a publisher. He writes, 'By the time I finished reading night had fallen, and it surprised me that the light was still on, that bread and tea were still available, that I didn't hear any airplanes droning overhead, nor any soldiers' boots stomping in the street – that is how captivated I was by what I had read, and how much it had taken me back to the insubstantial world that is already almost eight years behind us.' /

Het Parool, 3 April 1946

Red. en Adm.: A'dam-C. N.Z. Voorburgwal 225 Tel. 33232 Gem.-G. P10.000 Postgiro no. 260728. Ab. 31 ct. p. w. of f 4 p. kw Losse nummers 9 cent. Bankiers: Amst. Bank N.V., Bijkantoor Damrak.

HET PAROOL

VRIJ, ONVERVEERD

ONAFHANKELIJK DAGBLAD Uitgave van de Stichting Het Parool, Amsterdam Opgericht in 1940 door PIETER 't HOEN. Directeur: W. v. NORDEN

ZESDE JAARGANG No. 378 * Hoofdredacteur: Mr. G. J. van Heuven Goedhart. WOENSDAG 3 APRIL 1946

Kinderstem

DOOR een toeval heb ik een dagboek in handen gekregen, dat tijdens de oorlogsjaren geschreven is. Het Rijksinstituut voor Oorlogsdocumentatie bezit al omtrent 200 dergelijke dagboeken, maar het zou mij verbazen, als er daar nog één bij was, zóó zuiver, zóó intelligent, en toch zoo menschelijk als dit, dat ik het heden met zijn vele plichten voor één avond vergetend, in eenen gelezen heb.

Toen ik het uit had, was het nacht en het verwonderde mij, dat het licht nog brandde, dat er nog brood en thee te krijgen waren, dat ik geen vliegtuigen hoorde ronken en geen soldatenlaarzen klonken op straat, zóó had de lezing mij gevangen en teruggevoerd naar de onwezenlijke wereld, die nu al bijna weer een jaar achter ons ligt.

Het is geschreven door een Joodsch meisje, dat 13 jaar was, toen zij met haar ouders en een ouder zusje onderdook en dit dagboek begon en dat eindigt ruim twee jaar later, toen de Gestapo het gezin, op een onzaligen dag ontdekte. Eén maand voor de bevrijding is zij in een der ergste Duitsche concentratiekampen overleden nog vóór haar 16den verjaardag.

Hoe, daar wil ik mij niet in verdiepen. Maar het zal, staat te vreezen, zoo ongeveer geweest zijn als nu reeds in zooveel kampherinneringen te lezen staat, misschien wel zooals beschreven is in de onlangs verschenen brochure „Tusschen leven en dood in Auschwitz", al was het dan in een ander kamp.

De wijze van haar dood is ook niet belangrijk. Belangrijker was dit jonge leven dat moedwillig afgesneden werd door een systeem, welks geestelooze wreedheid wij elkaar wel is waar gezworen hebben nimmer te vergeten of te vergeven toen het nog woedde, maar dat wij desondanks, nu het voorbij is, toch reeds bezig zijn, zoo niet te vergeven dan toch te vergeten, wat uiteindelijk op hetzelfde neerkomt.

Voor mij echter is in dit schijnbaar onbeteekenende dagboek van een kind, in dit door een kinderstem gestamelde „de profundis" alle afzichtelijkheid van het fascisme belichaamd, méér dan in alle processtukken van Neurenberg bij elkaar. Voor mij is in het lot van dit Joodsche meisje de ergste misdaad saamgevat, die de eeuwig verfoeilijke geest beging. Want die ergste misdaad is niet de vernietiging van leven en cultuur op zichzelf: deze kunnen ook aan een cultuur scheppende [illegible] ten offer vallen, maar dat is het verstoppen van de bronnen der cultuur, de vernietiging van leven en [illegible] alleen uit domme vernietigingsdrift.

Dit meisje toch zou, als niet alle [illegible] een begaafde schrijfster geworden zijn als zij was blijven leven. Op haar vierde jaar uit Duitschland hierheen gekomen, schreef zij een jaar later reeds een benijdenswaardig zuiver en sober Nederlandsch en toont zij een inzicht in de feilen der menschelijke natuur — haar eigene niet uitgezonderd — zelf zóó feilloos, dat het nog verbaasd zou hebben in een volwassene, laat staan in een kind. Maar toont zij evenzeer de oneindige mogelijkheden dier zelfde menschelijke natuur, die in den humor, de deernis en de liefde gelegen zijn, waarover men zich misschien nog méér verwonderen moet en waarvoor men zelfs zou terugschrikken als voor al het zéér bijzondere, wanneer verwerping en aanvaarding niet tegelijk zoo innig-kinderlijk zouden zijn gebleven.

Dat dit meisje geroofd en gedood is kunnen worden, is voor mij het bewijs, dat wij den slag tegen het beest in den mensch verloren hebben. En we hebben dien verloren, omdat we er niets positiefs tegenover hebben gesteld. En daarom zullen we hem weer verliezen, in welken vorm de onmenschelijkheid ons ook belagen moge, wanneer we niet in staat blijken er alsnog iets positiefs tegenover te stellen. De belofte, dat wij nooit vergeten en vergeven zullen is niet voldoende. Het is zelfs niet voldoende die belofte te houden. Passieve en negatieve afweer is te weinig, is als niets. Actieve en positieve „totalitaire" democratie, politiek, sociaal, economisch en cultureel, zal het eenige redmiddel blijken: de opbouw van een maatschappij, waarin het talent niet langer vernietigd, verdrukt en verdrongen, maar ontdekt, gekweekt en voortgeholpen wordt, waar het zich ook maar voordoet. En van die democratie zijn we, met al onze goede [illegible] als vóór den oorlog.

J. ROMEIN

NA ZEVEN JAAR WEER JAARBEURS IN UTRECHT. — Duizenden waren gisteren, den dag der opening, aanwezig om deze heuglijke gebeurtenis in het Nederlandsche bedrijfsleven bij te wonen.

ER WORDEN WEER ORDERS GENOTEERD aan de stands op de Jaarbeurs in Utrecht.

De „Nieuw Amsterdam" komt thuis

Het vlaggeschip van de Holland-Amerikalijn, de „Nieuw Amsterdam", zal op 9 of 10 April na een afwezigheid van zes jaar in de haven Rotterdam terugkeeren. Het schip heeft 2289 repatrieerenden aan boord van Java en Colombo, en 700 man Engelsche troepen die te Southampton zullen debarkeeren.

Me[illegible]acht dat het schip in elk geval [illegible] avonduren zal aankomen. De [illegible] begint dan 's morgens om [illegible] uur.

Zeeuwsche Jaarbeurstrein

Op 9 April zal een extra trein voor Jaarbeursbezoekers uit Zeeland rijden. Deze trein vertrekt om 5 uur uit Vlissingen en is om 10.56 uur in Utrecht. Om 18.30 uur keert de trein naar Vlissingen terug, waar hij om 00.54 uur aankomt. Deze trein stopt 's morgens te 6.01 uur en 's nachts te 00.01 uur in Kruiningen—Ierseke.

De Bilt verwacht:

Aanvankelijk zwakken en veranderlijke wind met vrijwel onbewolkt weer. Behoudens plaatselijk mist. Later wind tusschen West en Zuid met eenige toeneming van bewolking, voornamelijk in het Noorden des lands. Droog weer. Weinig verandering van temperatuur.

Zon onder 19.15, op 6.09
Maan op 7.12, onder 21.06
5 April E.K.

Het onder de wapenen geroepen kader

Om alle voor uitzending naar Indonesië bestemde onderdeelen, enz. van kader te voorzien zijn sinds 17 September 1944, hetzij door vrijwillige aanmelding, hetzij door oproeping, in werkelijken dienst gekomen 10.898 onderofficieren en 4135 officieren. Dit deelde de minister van Oorlog mede naar aanleiding van de door het Kamerlid F. J. Goedhart gestelde vragen. In deze gevallen zijn niet begrepen de beroepsofficieren en beroepsonderofficieren en de officieren en onderofficieren met een tijdelijke aanstelling zonder vooropleiding. Voor vertrouwelijk gebruik, aldus de minister, zijn de richtlijnen voor het verleenen van vrijstellingen ter griffie der Tweede Kamer gedeponeerd. De minister kan in verband met den onzekeren toestand in Indonesië in plaats van een oproep „voor onbepaalden tijd" geen nauwkeuriger omschreven diensttijd aangeven.

Veiligheidsraad heden bijeen

Bonnet bemiddelaar?

(News Chronicle — Het Parool).

BYRNES werd gisteravond laat uit Washington, waar hij een onderhoud van een uur met President Truman had, in New York terug verwacht. Er was geen afspraak gemaakt voor een ontmoeting tusschen hem en Cadogan voor den aanvang van de zitting van den Veiligheidsraad. Wat precies gebeuren zal wanneer de Raad bijeenkomt en er geen antwoord van de Russen is, waagt niemand te voorspellen. Er is echter alle reden om aan te nemen, dat Byrnes en Cadogan zullen voortgaan met aan te dringen op een onmiddellijk onderzoek van de Perzische beschuldigingen. Hierin zullen zij zeker gesteund worden door verschillende andere gedelegeerden, o.w. Van Kleffens. De laage gedelegeerde van Polen zal waarschijnlijk verlenging vragen van de tijdslimiet voor de antwoorden. Het kan zijn, dat hij hierin gesteund wordt door Bonnet, die alsdan in deze zitting de bemiddelaarsrol tusschen Amerika en Rusland zou overnemen, die in Londen door Stettinius tusschen Bevin en Wisjinsky werd vervuld.

Alles zal echter voor een goed deel afhangen van den inhoud van het Perzische antwoord en of de Raad in zijn [illegible] het onderzoek van de Perzische klacht voort te gaan.

Kopenhagen in afwachting van Prinselijk Paar

Feestprogramma is opgesteld

(Van onzen Kopenhaagschen correspondent).

HET is geen gemeenplaats als ik zeg, dat het Nederlandsche en het Deensche volk nooit zoo innig met elkaar verbonden waren als [illegible] tijdens de vijf bezettingsjaren, onvergelijkelijk veel erger dan wat de Denen ondervonden, heeft een gevoel van groote sympathie doen ontstaan en het bezoek van prinses Juliana en prins Bernhard aan onze stad zal een schoone gelegenheid zijn, om daarvan blijk te geven.

De hooge Nederlandsche gasten zullen op uitdrukkelijk verlangen van koning Christiaan in zijn paleis hun intrek nemen. Vrijdagmorgen, onmiddellijk na hun aankomst op het vliegveld van Kopenhagen, zullen zij hun residentie betrekken, waar geluncht wordt. Na het door koning Christiaan te geven diner volgt een bezoek aan de Nederlandsche legatie. Zaterdag zullen alle Nederlandsche kinderen, die zich in Denemarken bevinden voor herstel van gezondheid, prinses Juliana, prins Bernhard en prinses Ingrid een aubade brengen, waarna de koninklijke gasten de leidende personen van de Deensche hulpverleening aan Nederland op de Nederlandsche legatie zullen ontvangen. Des avonds wordt te koninklijken paleize een gala-banquet gegeven; hier zullen ook de Deensche premier, de minister van Buitenlandsche Zaken en vele andere hooge personen aanwezig zijn. Zondag zal prins Bernhard namens de Nederlandsche verzetsbeweging een krans leggen op het massagraf der door de Duitschers gefusilleerde Deensche verzetsmannen. Des avonds geeft het Concertgebouw uitsluitend voor genoodigden zijn eerste concert. Uitgevoerd worden de Ouverture Egmond en de Vijfde Symphonie van Tschaikowsky. Maandag wordt een voor het publiek toegankelijk concert gegeven.

Voor het vertrek, dat op Maandag is vastgesteld, brengt het prinselijk paar, evenals Koningin Wilhelmina bij haar laatste bezoek aan Denemarken deed, een bezoek aan het eilandje Amager tegenover Kopenhagen gelegen, om een kijkje te nemen bij eenige van de 3000 afstammelingen van Nederlanders, die daar in 1521 op verzoek van een Deenschen koning een nederzetting vormden, ter vestiging van een intensieve groentecultuur [illegible] hebben nog altijd hun oude gewoonten en kleedij. Aan den ingang van [illegible] ters in historische uniformen de prinses en den prins ontvangen en rondleiden, welk bezoek met een Nederlandschen kerkdienst wordt besloten.

De hooge gasten vertrekken dan per vliegtuig naar Stockholm, waar evenééns een uitvoerig feestprogram op hen wacht.

Met Paschen een ei

Op 8 April a.s. zal voor Paschen een bon voor een ei (alle leeftijdsgroepen) aangewezen worden, welke bon drie weken geldig zal blijven. De verstrekking zal echter geleidelijk geschieden, hetgeen voor een groot deel van de medewerking der legkippen afhangt. Van een regelmatige, algemeene distributie zal vooreerst nog geen sprake kunnen zijn.

Wilde staking bij Hartog en Zwanenberg te Oss

Bij de vleeschbedrijven van de N.V. Hartog en de N.V. Zwanenberg te Oss zijn gisteren circa 700 arbeiders in wilde staking gegaan, aangezien de nieuwe door het college van Rijksbemiddelaars per 1 Januari 1946 vastgestelde loonen nog niet waren uitbetaald, zoodat de arbeiders een loonvordering bezaten. De directie verklaarde deze loonen niet te kunnen uitbetalen, zoolang niet was vastgesteld, welke arbeiders tot de ongeschoolde, geoefende en geschoolde werkkrachten moesten worden gerekend. Zij weigerde allen arbeiders een voorschot van f 100.— te verstrekken.

Thans heeft de directie de fabrieks[illegible] verschuldigde achterstallige loon vanaf 1 Januari 1946 zal worden uitgekeerd. Aan de overige arbeiders zal een voorloopig bedrag van f 30 bij wijze van voorschot worden uitbetaald. Door deze maatregelen hoopt men de arbeiders zoo spoedig mogelijk weer aan het werk te krijgen.

Meeste ontsnappingen uit Vught

Van de meer dan honderdduizend politieke gedetineerden, sinds de bevrijding in bewaring gesteld, is, voornamelijk in de eerste maanden der bevrijding, 0,06% ontsnapt, aldus deelde de minister van Justitie mede, in antwoord op door den heer Van der Goes van Naters gestelde vragen. Een vierde deel hiervan ontvluchtte uit Vught. De oorzaak hiervan is, dat dit kamp tot voor kort mede bij de geallieerden in gebruik was, waardoor contrôle minder gemakkelijk was. De ontvluchtingen moeten geweten worden aan de ongeschikte inrichting der kampen en gebrek aan scholing van het bewakingspersoneel. Naar verbetering wordt gestreefd.

Duizend monteerbare huizen (z.g. „prefabricated houses") zullen uit Engeland naar Nederland worden geëxporteerd. — (U.P.)

Engelsche anti-stakingswet thans ingetrokken

ONDER daverende en langdurige [illegible] digden der Arbeiderspartij heeft het Engelsche Lagerhuis met 349 tegen 182 stemmen de gehate „Trades Dispute Act" ingetrokken, welke een algemeene staking onwettig verklaarde en het lidmaatschap van vakvereenigingen en de Arbeiderspartij voor ambtenaren verbood.

Deze wet, die buitengewoon gehaat was bij de arbeiders, werd in 1926 na de algemeene staking door de conservatieve regeering ingediend en door het parlement aanvaard. Zij bepaalde o.a., dat een lid van een vakvereeniging, wanneer hij wenschte, dat van zijn contributie een deel werd afgestaan aan een politieke organisatie, dit uitdrukkelijk moest vermelden. Voordien — en dus thans ook weer — was het de gewoonte, dat automatisch een deel der contributies aan de Labour-partij werd afgedragen en de leden, die dit niet wenschten, moesten dit uitdrukkelijk vermelden. De wet werd algemeen beschouwd als een strafmaatregel wegens de algemeene staking van 1926.

De intrekking van de wet maakt een algemeene staking echter nog niet wettig: dit moet nu nog geregeld worden.

„De oude vakvereenigingsmenschen hebben twintig jaar op deze stemming [illegible] cie". Hun toejuichingen bewezen, dat zij de stemming als een historische gebeurtenis beschouwden. De geheele linksche pers juicht natuurlijk, doch de conservatieve bladen beschuldigen Labour er van haar meerderheid op „dictatoriale wijze" te gebruiken.

Oproep van Partij van den Arbeid

De Partij van den Arbeid heeft zich met een Oproep tot het Nederlandsche volk gericht in verband met de a.s. verkiezingen voor de Tweede Kamer, Provinciale Staten en gemeenteraden, welke zullen beslissen over den koers, dien 't bevrijde Nederland zal gaan. Zooals wij tijdens de bezetting in gemeenschappelijke verantwoordelijkheid stand hebben gehouden tegen de tyrannie van het nationaal-socialisme, aldus luidt de oproep, zoo is het nu onze plicht om in gemeenschappelijke verantwoordelijkheid in een nieuwe wereld gestalte te geven aan een nieuw Nederland en aan het Koninkrijk op nieuwen grondslag. Deze opbouw zal slechts kunnen slagen, wanneer hij gedragen wordt door een herstel van de zedelijke waarden; wanneer de persoonlijke vrijheid en verantwoordelijkheid voldoende zijn gewaarborgd tegen de gevaren van ieder staatsabsolutisme; wanneer de ordening van het maatschappelijk leven gestuwd wordt door een wil tot consequente sociale gerechtigheid. De Partij van den Arbeid meent, dat een doorbreking der vruchteloos geworden politieke scheidslijnen dringend is geboden en streeft er naar om alle vooruitstrevende krachten uit de verschillende godsdienstige en maatschappelijke kringen te vereenigen op een program van constructief socialisme. Zij gaat daarom de verkiezingen in met het thans definitief geworden urgentieprogram, dat destijds reeds in ontwerp was vastgelegd voordat de Partij van den Arbeid was geconstitueerd.

Liberalen stellen geen candidaten

De algemeene vergadering van de Liberale Staatspartij heeft besloten, bij de a.s. verkiezingen geen candidaten te stellen, maar samen te werken met de Partij van de Vrijheid en de candidaten van deze partij te steunen.

Prof. dr. S. de Boer berispt

De minister van O. K. en W. heeft prof. dr. S. de Boer berispt wegens zijn houding gedurende de bezetting en zijn schorsing als hoogleeraar aan de rijksuniversiteit te Groningen opgeheven.

Baron Van Asbeck zal binnenkort naar Java vertrekken, ten einde dr. Idenburg, directeur van het kabinet van den lt.-gouverneur-generaal voor een periode van drie maanden in deze functie te vervangen.

Gromyko heeft gisteravond op een vraag, of hij de bijeenkomst van den Veiligheidsraad zou bijwonen, „neen" geantwoord. Hij weigerde zijn antwoord nader toe te lichten, aldus meldt Reuter.

— Bevin heeft meegedeeld, dat hij voornemens is binnenkort naar Egypte te gaan voor het bijwonen der Engelsch-Britsche onderhandelingen.

DEZE ZOMER OPROEPING NIEUWE LICHTINGEN

In Mei en October zullen de lichtingen 1945 en 1946 onder de wapenen worden geroepen, in totaal ter sterkte van ongeveer 60.000 man, aldus heeft de minister van Oorlog, J. Meynen, in zijn antwoord op de vragen van het Tweede-Kamerlid L. F. Duymaer van Twist verklaard. Voor zoover thans is te voorzien zullen zij bestemd zijn voor uitzending naar Indonesië.

De troepen, die thans in Nederland dienst doen, zijn samengesteld uit vrijwilligers, die niet bereid gevonden zijn de oorlogsverbandakte te teekenen, en dus niet naar Indonesië kunnen worden uitgezonden. Zij zullen in den loop van 1946 worden gedemobiliseerd.

KAARSEN VRIJ.

Kaarsen zullen voortaan weder zonder bon in den detailhandel verkrijgbaar zijn, zij het nog niet in onbeperkte hoeveelheden.

De Communistische Partij Nederland zal voor de Tweede Kamerverkiezingen twintig candidaten stellen. De voornaamste zijn: Gerben Wagenaar, Paul de Groot, C. Borst, A. C. Koenen, mr. B. J. Stokvis, J. Hoogcarspel, Brecht v. d. Muijzenberg geb. Willemse, Jef Spijkers, Jan Haken en Fred. Schoonenberg.

Sjahrir en Kerr uiten zich beiden optimistisch

SJAHRIR heeft in een interview, dat hij gisteren volgens A.N.P.-Aneta toestond aan de plaatselijke bladen te Batavia, zijn voldoening uitgesproken over de vorderingen, die tot dusver bij de onderhandelingen met de Nederlanders zijn gemaakt, maar hij wees er op, dat nog veel overkoepeld moest worden. Het concept, waarover hij en zijn collega's en de Nederlandsche vertegenwoordigers het eens zijn geworden, moet nog onder de oogen gezien worden door de Nederlandsche regeering en zal mogelijk ook door de Indonesische regeering bestudeerd moeten worden.

Sjahrir hoopte, dat het resultaat van de onderhandelingen zou zijn, dat Indonesië in staat zal zijn, zijn plaats onder de andere naties in te nemen en lid te worden van de organisatie der Vereenigde Naties. Hij verklaarde, dat hoewel de Indonesiërs niet denken dat de U.N.O. iets volmaakts was, zij verlangend waren deel te nemen aan haar werkzaamheden en te arbeiden voor haar volmaaktheid.

Ook sir Archibald Clark Kerr heeft verklaard voldaan te zijn over het resultaat der onderhandelingen, die volgens hem niet zoo zeer moeilijk dan wel traag waren. Hij zeide tot de Indonesische journalisten: „De kwestie Nederland-Indonesië is een interne aangelegenheid. Hoewel andere landen de verplichtingen hebben bijstand te verleenen, hebben Groot-Brittannië en Amerika geen verlangen op economisch gebied ten aanzien van Indonesië."

Een conferentie, welke naar men meent de slotbijeenkomst tusschen de Britten en de Indonesische republikeinsche autoriteiten over kwesties, die betrekking hebben op de evacuatie van Japanners en bevrijde geïnterneerden uit het binnenland, zal zijn, is thans in het geallieerde hoofdkwartier aan den gang.

— Na 45 dienstjaren is de hoofddirecteur van Personeele Zaken van het hoofdbestuur der P.T.T. te Den Haag, de heer A. van Veen, met pensioen gegaan. De heer Van Veen is oud-directeur van het postkantoor te Amsterdam geweest. De Amsterdamsche Postharmonie bracht hem een aubade.

Otto Frank types out a portion of Anne's writings. He hopes to find a publisher. Otto tries to carry out Anne's wish that her diary be published, and he sends typescripts to several publishers in the Netherlands.

Pseudonyms in *Het Achterhuis*:
Hermann van Pels =
Mr (Hermann) Van Daan
Auguste van Pels =
Mrs (Petronella) Van Daan
Peter van Pels =
Peter van Daan
Fritz Pfeffer =
Mr (Albert) Dussel
Victor Kugler =
Mr (Harry) Kraler
Johannes Kleiman =
Mr (Simon) Koophuis
Bep Voskuijl =
Elli Vossen
Miep Gies =
Miep van Santen
Jan Gies =
Henk van Santen

Het Achterhuis is published on 25 June 1947. The cover is the work of designer Helmut Salden. It features a sun disappearing behind dark clouds.

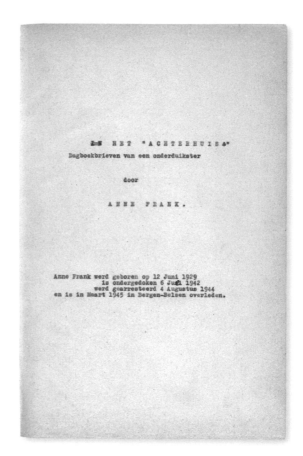

As a result of this glowing article, the publisher Contact expresses interest in publishing the diary of Anne Frank. Otto puts together a book from Anne's texts and gives it the title she herself had thought up: *Het Achterhuis*. Otto uses some of the names from Anne's list of pseudonyms, but others he makes up himself.

On 25 June 1947 *Het Achterhuis* is published. The Dutch edition is followed by translations in more than seventy different languages, along with stage plays and numerous films. Books about Anne Frank come out every year, and there seems to be no end to the new films and plays being produced.

On 10 November 1953 Otto Frank marries Fritzi Geiringer. From left to right: Johannes Kleiman, Jan Gies, Fritzi Frank-Geiringer, Otto Frank, Johanna Kleiman (wife of Johannes), and Miep Gies.

The hiding place where Anne did most of her writing has been a museum since 1960: the Anne Frank House. Otto Frank is closely involved in the museum's founding. He realises early on how important a visit to the empty Secret Annexe can be.

Otto Frank also wants to bring young people to Amsterdam from all over the world for special summer conferences, lectures, and courses. During the conferences young people discuss current themes such as 'the youth in a changing world' and 'religion in the world of today'. The courses focus on the dialogue between Judaism and Christianity, for example.

The view of the chestnut tree from Anne Frank's room in 1958. Young Germans from Hamburg have left a commemorative wreath with text *'In stillem Gedenken'* (In silent remembrance).

Otto Frank does not want any furniture in the Secret Annexe because the Annexe was completely cleared after the arrest by order of the German occupiers. In 1961 he does commission the construction of two detailed models of the two floors of the Annexe: the floor of the Van Pels family and the floor of the Frank family and Fritz Pfeffer. Otto Frank hopes the models will give visitors a better idea of the conditions under which the inhabitants lived.

'After the Anne Frank House was restored, they asked me whether the rooms should be furnished or not. But I answered, "No. Everything was removed during the war and I want it to stay that way." But after the opening, some people who visited the House thought the rooms were very spacious. I told them their impression was incorrect, and I said: Don't forget the unbearable tension we lived under, when all eight of us were living in the one large room.' (Otto Frank, *Het Vrije Volk*, 24 May 1962)'

Although Otto Frank makes his home in Basel, Switzerland, in 1952, he closely follows the developments in Amsterdam in his function as board member. He also generously supports the activities of the Anne Frank House with proceeds from the sale of the diary.

Otto and his second wife Fritzi receive thousands of letters from readers of the diary. He talks about this in an interview: 'Young people in particular are eager to know more and more about how such terrible events could ever have taken place. I answer them as best I can. And at the end I often write, "I hope Anne's book will have a lasting effect on you in later life, so that you too will work for reconciliation and peace, as far as your circumstances will allow."' /

Anne Frank Stichting, *Anne Frank,* 1979

Until his death in 1980, Otto dedicates himself to working for a better world, which was Anne's wish. 'I am almost ninety now and my strength is gradually declining. But the task that Anne set before me keeps giving me new strength – to struggle for reconciliation and for human rights the world over.' /

Welt am Sonntag, 4 February 1979

Otto Frank speaking
with Israeli young
people, 1966.

Het Achterhuis has
now been translated
into more the seventy
languages.

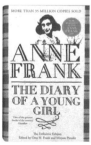

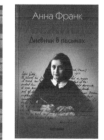

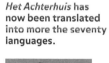

Otto Frank in the attic
of the Secret Annexe
a few hours before
the official opening
of the Anne Frank
House on 3 May 1960.

SOURCES QUOTED

The following sources were used in this book:

Anne Frank House – www.annefrank.org, 2016.

Anne Frank House / Metselaar, Menno – *'Ik had geen idee dat zij dat allemaal op zou schrijven'* ['I had no idea she was writing everything down'], interview with Miep Gies, *Anne Frank Magazine*, 1998.

Anne Frank House / Metselaar, Menno – *'God weet alles, maar Anne weet het beter'* ['God knows all, but Anne knows better'], interview with Hannah Goslar, *Anne Frank Magazine*, 1998.

Anne Frank Stichting (eds.) – *Anne Frank*, Amsterdam: Keesing Boeken, 1979.

Anonymous – Joint meeting of the N.S.D.A.P. and N.S.B. in Breda, *De Residentiebode*, 29 June 1942.

Bretz, Alice – *I Begin Again*, New York: McGraw-Hill Book Company, 1940.

Frank, Anne – *Original diary manuscripts, versions A and B, 1942 – 1944.*

Frank, Anne – *Verhalen rondom het achterhuis* [Stories from the Secret Annexe], Amsterdam: Contact, 1960.

Frank, Otto – *Anne's World*, Anne Frank House, 2010.

Frank, Otto – *Anne Franks Vater: „Ich will Versöhnung"* [Anne Frank's father: 'I would like reconciliation'], article in *Welt am Sonntag*, 4 February 1979.

Frank, Otto – *Maquette van het Achterhuis.* [Model of the Secret Annex] article in *Het Vrije Volk*, 24 May 1962.

Gies, Miep - *Anne Frank Remembered: The Story of the Woman who Helped to Hide the Frank Family*, New York: Simon & Schuster, 1987.

Kienzle, Birgit (Director) – *Lasst mich so sein wie ich will. Anne Frank* [Let be me myself. Anne Frank], documentary, Südwestfunk, 1979.

Lindwer, Willy – *The Last Seven Months of Anne Frank,* translated by Alison Meersschaert, London: Young Picador, 2004.

NIOD – *The Diary of Anne Frank: The Critical Edition,* New York: Doubleday, 1989.

Romein, Jan – *Kinderstem* [A child's voice], article in *Het Parool*, 3 April 1946.

Schnabel, Ernst – *Footsteps of Anne Frank*, translated by Richard and Clara Winston, London: Southbank Publishing, 2015.

Winter-Levy, de, Rosa – *Aan de gaskamer ontsnapt! Het Satanswerk van de SS.* [Escape from the gas chamber! The satanic work of the SS], Doetinchem: Uitgevers-mij "C. Misset", 1945.

Wirtz, Gérard – *Wir sind bewusstere Juden geworden* [As Jews, we have become more conscious of our identity], Interview with Otto Frank, *Basler Magazin*, 24 February 1979.

PHOTO CREDITS

The Anne Frank House has made every effort to identify the rightful claimants to the photographs in this book . If you believe nonetheless that your rights have not been honoured, please contact us.

t=top; **b**=bottom; **l**=left; **r**=right; **c**=centre

Akg Images – pg 194

Akg Images/Hans Asemissen – pg 18

Akg Images/Walter Ballhause – pg 15t

Beeldbank WO2/NIOD – pgs 17b, 21b, 145t, 145b, 148tl, 148tr, 148b, 150tl, 150b, 179t, 179b, 180t

Beeldbank WO2/NIOD - Mr. A. Hustinx Collection – pgs 20c, 21t, 197b

Beeldbank WO2/Resistance Museum Amsterdam – pgs. 146-147

bpk Bildagentur/Helmut Schäfer – pg 20t

bpk Bildagentur /Karl H. Paulmann – pg 19t

Bundesarchiv, Bild P049500 – pg 15b

City Archives, Amsterdam/Frits Rotgans – pg 144b

Diederik Schiebergen – pgs 22br, 108, 143b, 180b

FOTO Aviodrome, Lelystad – pgs 2-3

Getty Images / Time LIFE Picture Collection, courtesy of Hugo Jäger – pgs 19b, 20b

Getty Images/© Arnold Newman – pg 206

Getty Images/ Heritage Collection – pg 195

Herinneringscentrum Kamp Westerbork – pg 170

Hollandse Hoogte/Corbis – pg 197t

Imperial War Museum – pgs 183t, 183b, 184t, 184b, 185, 186

Maria Austria Institute / MAI – pgs 4, 66t, 68, 71bl, 71br, 79t, 79b, 86t, 100b, 101t, 101b, 117b, 120b, 200

Nederlands Fotomuseum/Carel Blazer – pg 1

Nederlands Fotomuseum/Cas Oorthuys – pgs 22t, 149

Nederlands Fotomuseum/Ed van der Elsken – pg 203b

Nederlands Fotomuseum/City Archive, Utrecht/Nico Jesse – pgs 22bl, 144t

Panstwowe Muzeum Auschwitz-Birkenau – pg 182b

Photo Collection Anne Frank House, Amsterdam – pgs 8, 16, 17t, 29, 30-31, 32, 33t, 33b, 34-35, 36l, 36r, 37, 38, 39, 40l, 40r, 41, 42, 43, 44, 52l, 52r, 53, 54-55, 56, 57t, 57b, 58, 66b, 69, 70, 72b, 80-81, 82tl, 82tr, 83, 86b, 93, 94-95, 96, 97t, 97b, 100t, 104t, 105t, 105bl, 105br, 106t, 106b, 107t, 107b, 115, 116bl, 116br, 117t, 118, 121t, 122, 129, 130, 131, 132, 133, 134, 135, 136t, 136b, 143t, 157, 158-159, 160, 161, 162, 163, 164l, 164r, 165l, 165r, 166-167, 168, 169t, 169b, 171, 198t, 198c, 198b, 201, 202t, 202b, 203t, 204, 205

Photo Collection Anne Frank House, Amsterdam/ Allard Bovenberg – pgs 65, 67t, 67b, 71t, 72t, 82b, 84-85, 98-99, 102-103, 104b, 116t, 119t, 119b, 120t, 121b

Photo Collection Anne Frank House, Amsterdam/ Hans van den Heuvel – pg 5

The Wiener Library/courtesy of Ruth Wiener – pg 172

United States Holocaust Memorial Museum/courtesy of Penny Boyer – pg 51

www.ssmaritime.com – pg 196

Yad Vashem – pgs 181t, 181b, 182t

Colophon

**Published and produced by
The Anne Frank House**

Copyright © 2016
Anne Frank Stichting, Amsterdam

Text
Anne Frank House (Menno Metselaar)

Project Management
Anne Frank House (Tom Brink)

Project Coordination
Anne Frank House (Eugenie Martens)

Historical research and supervision
Anne Frank House (Erika Prins)

Photo research
Anne Frank House (Karolien Stocking Korzen)

Production support
Anne Frank House (Erica Terpstra)

Editing
Mieke Sobering

Final edit
Vos|seo tekst & web (Gerti Vos, Ingrid Mersel)

Design & Typesetting
Joseph Plateau Graphic Design

Translation
Forest-Flier Editorial Services (Nancy Forest-Flier)

Illustrated cross section of the Anne Frank House
Vizualism (Chantal van Wessel, Frédérik Ruys)

Lithography
Colorset (Marion Pothoff)

Printing
Zwaan Printmedia

Second edition, February 2017 (in Dutch, English,
German, French, Spanish, Italian and Portuguese)
ISBN/EAN: 978-90-8667-067-3

anne frank house

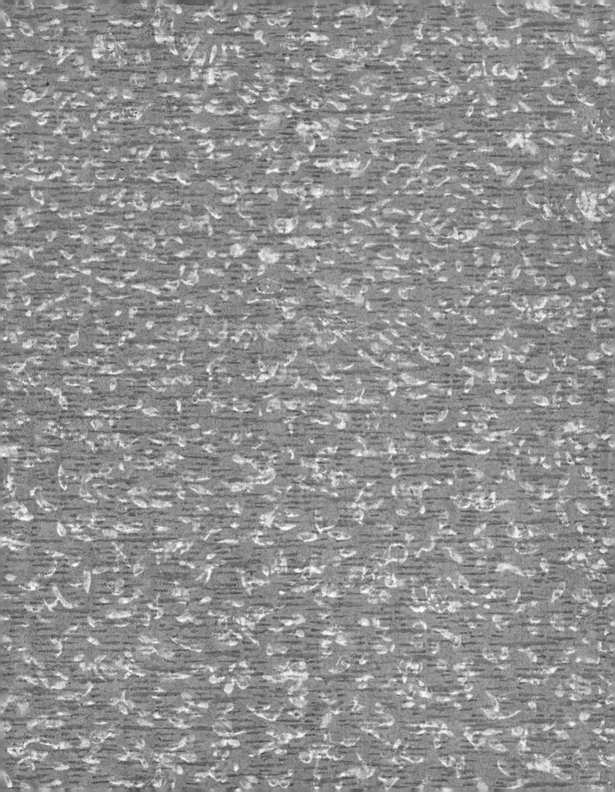